Farm Journal's
Great Dishes from the Oven

Other cookbooks by FARM JOURNAL

Farm Journal's
Great Dishes from the Oven

By Rita Holmberg with the
Food Editors of Farm Journal

SIMON AND SCHUSTER
New York

Published by Simon and Schuster,
A Division of Gulf & Western Corporation
Simon & Schuster Building
Rockefeller Center
1230 Avenue of the Americas
New York, New York 10020

Published in association with Countryside Press,
A Division of Farm Journal, Inc.

Designed by Maureen Sweeney

Manufactured in the United States of America

Library of Congress Catalog Card
Number 77-80775

ISBN 0-671-24039-0
First Edition

Contents

CHAPTER I

Make the Most of Your Oven

If you're like most homemakers, you use your oven almost every day—for savory brown roasts, tender oven-fried or braised meats and poultry, hearty casseroles, breads of all kinds, scrumptious cookies and desserts. There are many advantages in using your oven especially on extra-busy days when you don't have time to spend hours in the kitchen. Everyone is concerned about excess use of energy these days. Many homemakers have been extravagant in the use of oven heat. These are some of the extravagances:

• Putting a casserole "solo" into an oven which has plenty of room to accommodate a hot bread and a baked dessert, too.

• Preheating an oven much longer than is necessary to reach the required temperature.

• Turning on a 30-inch oven to warm a roll or two.

• Baking a single pan of muffins when another pan, or a loaf of quick bread, might be baked alongside, then stored in the freezer for later use.

Oven Management

In order to use your oven to the best advantage you will have to do some advance planning. Consider your family's living and eating patterns, their work schedules and the way you entertain. It does take *management* to make the oven work for you. But the pay-off is worth the effort in time, energy and money saved.

Oven Meals

Oven meals are one of the best possible ways to use your oven efficiently—plan on baking most of the meal (except for salad and beverage) in the oven. Many quick-cooking vegetables lend themselves to top-of-the-range cooking. However, others such as potatoes, winter squash, carrots, parsnips and onions bake to perfection in the oven.

Perhaps you have limited oven meals to everyday meals for the family. The oven can produce great company meals, too. In addition to saving time and money, you will have more time to visit with your guests.

Build your meal around a meat, fish or poultry recipe. Let the baking temperature and time for the main dish be the guide for the rest of the meal. Ideally, all foods for an oven meal ought to require the same temperature and baking time. However, a 25-degree difference in temperature isn't serious and, if timing does vary, plan to start some foods later or remove them earlier when done. One of the beauties of many baked foods is their great holding quality.

You can also shorten cooking time for a specific companion oven dish in a number of ways. For example, slice or dice or cut vegetables in strips instead of leaving them whole. Shape individual meat loaves rather than one large loaf. Bake puddings in custard cups.

As a general rule, meat dishes and vegetables bake more evenly on the bottom oven rack, while desserts and quick breads turn out best when cooked on the upper rack. Place unfilled utensils in the oven before you prepare the meal, to be sure they fit. For best heat circulation, they should not touch, nor should one utensil be placed directly over another.

When You Entertain

You can use your oven for all types of entertaining situations—hearty snack times, luncheons, light suppers and brunches. Build your menu around a make-ahead chili, lasagne or chicken crepes which you refrigerate or freeze. It's ready to slide in the oven to bake while you enjoy the party. Pop a make-ahead bread and dessert in the oven, too, to complete a menu.

A particular hit with young people are "packet burgers" or "packet chicken". These favorite foods are cooked in foil pouches, then served piping hot right from the pouch. And best of all no dishes to wash!

Cooking Double

Follow the popular "cook once for twice" practice by roasting meat or poultry in an amount sufficient to supply enough for two or possibly three meals. Perhaps you have tried this method with turkey and ham, but have you ever tried it with corned beef—the kind processed for oven roasting—or with a large pork roast? The "dividend" meat dishes are as delicious as the first-day roast when made into casseroles, creamed dishes or sandwiches. And the time and money you'll save is an extra bonus.

If you're not planning to use the roast meat within a few days, wrap it securely and tuck it away in the freezer—the shorter the time there, the better. Remove excess fat and bone from large pieces. Then wrap in heavy duty foil or moisture-vapor proof plastic bags, label and freeze. The foil or plastic will protect against drying and loss of flavor and color. Then use within a month or two.

Add water to the bones, with the meat which adheres to them, salt and pepper and a little minced onion. Simmer slowly for a flavorful broth and freeze for later use.

Place slices or small pieces of meat in plastic containers or foil pans and cover with broth, gravy or sauce to fill space and prevent drying by exposure of surfaces to air. The meat will hold well for 2 to 4 months.

If you should want to freeze either roast meat or poultry with the bone still in, the newer extra-heavy duty foil will be a good choice, since it's strong and particularly resistant to piercing or tearing.

With a few packages of roast meat or poultry in the freezer, you can come up with any number of interesting dishes. If you have frozen broth on hand as well, your options are further increased.

Dishes for Toting

If you're often asked to tote a main dish to a potluck, a family reunion or a church supper, it helps considerably to have several of your choice main dishes prepared in advance and stashed in the freezer.

Since dishes you carry generally run to the large, economy size, they require rather long heating time if the mixture is frozen. To cut that time, transfer the frozen dish to the refrigerator ahead of time for almost complete thawing before putting it in the oven.

When you're preparing a generous-sized casserole for a group gathering, why not make 1½ times the recipe and freeze the extra amount in individual portions? Nice to have on hand when someone in the family needs a substantial snack outside the regularly scheduled mealtime, or for quick, easy heating by the family when you're away from home.

Fresh-baked Breads and Cookies

In general, breads and cookies, those two oven products so popular with all age groups, are at their very best when freshly baked. (Fruit and nut loaves and a few special cookies which mellow on storage are exceptions.)

Thanks to efficient freezers, that "fresh-baked" quality can be preserved briefly (on long storage it's lost). Also, breads and cookies are bulky and fill space which you might use to better advantage for some other food. The solution? Bake more often, freeze for short periods, and enjoy top-quality eating.

Consider the idea of concentrating your baking activity into one block of time—maybe a morning or an afternoon. Or plan it for an evening, when volunteers can help with the measuring and mixing (and enjoy the good eating returns!). You can make it a real "Bake-In" and turn out an assortment of your family's favorite breads and cookies in production-line fashion.

A large part of the success of your project will be in the planning and organization beforehand. Review your recipes, check oven temperatures and timings, and choose those breads and cookies which can be prepared and baked to most efficiently use the oven heat and space. Line up ingredients, and clear the decks for efficient work space. Then systematize the sifting, measuring, chopping, etc. to save time. Dovetail the baking, to keep that oven full.

You may want to mix some of the cookies and freeze them as doughs, to bake later, and take advantage of an oven you've heated for something else. The dough requires less storage space than baked cookies and you can can turn out a batch of "fresh-baked" cookies in a few minutes when unexpected guests drop in. Breads and rolls are generally better when frozen after they're baked.

Cool breads and cookies thoroughly before packaging for the freezer. Package breads in moisture-vapor proof wrap or bags, seal tightly and label. Tender coffee cakes or rings need the protection of a rigid base, or packaging in a plastic container or cardboard carton.

Package cookies in plastic or metal containers with tight-fitting lids, to prevent flavor and moisture loss and avoid breaking and crushing.

Use frozen breads and cookies while they're in top condition. Breads *can* be kept in the freezer from 3 months to a year, but they're at their best if used within 3 months. Cookies, either baked or unbaked, are good keepers—9 to 12 months is their recommended storage time.

Delectable Desserts

Use your oven to prepare an interesting variety of make-ahead desserts to have on hand in the freezer, ready to serve at any time: fruit and chiffon pies, cakes, Alaska-type desserts, tortes. Bake pie or tart shells or rounds or squares of pastry to freeze and have on hand to use with prepared fruit or cream filling, or with ice cream and a yummy topping.

When apples, berries, peaches or other fruits are in peak supply, bank their flavorful goodness for off-season enjoyment. Make and freeze pies to bake later. Or prepare fillings and freeze them, to put together with pie crust or cobbler dough just before baking.

As with breads and cookies, desserts will be most enjoyed if not stored over-long. Since they're space-eaters, too, they can become costly to freeze, so you will not want to amass a surplus of them.

The "Good for You" Angle

Follow the oven route and you'll be able to enhance the nutritional value of the food you prepare. You'll use less fat by baking meats, fish or poultry than you would by pan-frying, and so will save on calories. You can bake vegetables like potatoes and winter squash, and fruits like apples and pears, with their skins on, and get the bonus of added minerals and vitamins. By using whole-grain flours, you can step up the nutrients and the flavor of baked goods.

Handy Oven Design Features

Make the most of the helpful design features your particular range might have. The handy minute timer, which buzzes or rings at the exact time you select makes clock watching unnecessary; the glass door, which cuts down on frequent opening and shutting during baking and the resultant loss of oven heat; the automatic meat thermometer, which gives you an accurate reading of the internal temperature of meat or poultry as it roasts.

A feature on many electric ranges is the automatic clock, which allows you to prepare a meal several hours in advance, place it in the oven, set the time cooking is to start, and let the range take over for you while you're out of the kitchen.

On gas ranges, this same type of delayed start may be available, or you may find a cook and keep warm programmed control.

This feature varies in operation from one model to another, so it's wise to consult the Use Booklet which comes with your range for specific instructions.

The delayed cooking feature is convenient, indeed! You don't use it for foods which should be started in a preheated oven, of course. And, for safety's sake, be sure the foods you put in the oven are thoroughly chilled or frozen if they're to remain for several hours before cooking begins, *especially during hot weather.*

Never—in any kind of weather—include milk and egg mixtures in automatically cooked meals. Such mixtures should be kept well chilled until cooking time. Held in a room temperature oven, they provide an ideal medium for bacterial growth and, almost inevitably, food poisoning.

Certainly the most welcomed design feature of all time has been the oven that cleans itself, which can be one of two types. In a self-cleaning oven (pyrolytic), soil is reduced to a light ash during a separate high-heat cycle. In a continuous-cleaning oven (catalytic), the oven walls or panels are specially treated so that soil is gradually reduced to a presentably clean condition during normal baking or roasting operations. Both systems help eliminate one of the most universally disliked of all household tasks.

The cleaning feature is particularly worthwhile when the oven is used frequently for roasting, or broiling meats.

You undoubtedly have your own tricks for using your oven to the maximum, and you'll come up with others as you think about it. Put them together with the ideas in this book, and develop a whole new repertoire of scrumptious food from the oven!

CHAPTER II

Family Meals From the Oven

Who's more interested in good food than a hungry family at the end of a busy day? You'll give yourself a head start on appreciative comments if you build oven meals around some of your family's favorite main dishes.

Many of these will already be oven dishes and the others can easily be adapted from top-of-range to oven cooking. To complete the menu, choose foods that will keep them company in the oven.

If baking times of all the foods don't match precisely, no problem. They needn't all be put into the oven at the same time as long as they come out in time for the meal. For example, you may wish to start a fruit crisp ahead of the main dish and remove it from the oven so that it can be served at perfect temperature—gently warm.

Some winter vegetables, such as rutabagas, parsnips, white and sweet potatoes and onions are especially suited for oven baking. Other vegetables can be turned into oven dishes by scalloping, saucing or by making them into a souffle or pudding, for example.

Certain frozen vegetables can be cooked in the oven as well as top-of-range. Add butter or margarine, your favorite seasonings (try new ones from time to time) and just enough water or broth to prevent sticking. Cover and let bake to tender crispness . . . less trouble than watching them in a skillet.

After you've tried the following meals, jot down some of your family's favorite dishes, with their bak-

15

ing temperatures and times. Then mix and match menus to create appetizing and easy-to-prepare oven meals.

MENU I

Beef Short Ribs and Rice *
Parslied Whole Carrots *
Tomato Aspic
Sesame English Muffins *
Baked Pears with Marshmallow Sauce *
Beverage

* Recipes given

Hearty short ribs and rice slowly bake in a 325° oven for 2 hours; carrots and pears, for less time. After removing the main meal, "up" the oven to 500°. Quickly prepare the Sesame Muffins and toast lightly.

BEEF SHORT RIBS AND RICE

---

4 lbs. beef short ribs, cut in squares
1 c. regular rice
½ c. chopped onion
½ c. chopped celery
½ c. chopped green pepper
1 tblsp. salt
⅛ tsp. pepper
½ tsp. thyme leaves
2½ c. water
2 tsp. instant beef bouillon powder
1 tsp. Worcestershire sauce

Slowly brown short ribs on all sides in heavy Dutch oven. Remove meat. Add rice, onion, celery and green pepper. Cook, stirring occasionally, until rice is lightly browned.

Turn rice mixture into 3-qt. casserole and top with browned ribs. Combine salt, pepper, thyme, water, bouillon and Worcestershire sauce. Pour over meat. Cover.

Bake in 325° oven about 2 hours or until meat is tender. Makes 6 servings.

PARSLIED WHOLE CARROTS

---

8 to 10 medium carrots, pared
½ c. water
¾ tsp. salt
⅛ tsp. pepper
½ tsp. sugar
2 tblsp. butter
1 tblsp. chopped fresh parsley

Place carrots in 9-inch square baking dish. Combine water, salt, pepper and sugar; pour over carrots. Dot with butter. Cover.

Bake in 325° oven 1 to 1¼ hours or until tender. Drain, if necessary. Sprinkle with parsley. Makes 6 servings.

SESAME ENGLISH MUFFINS

---

6 English muffins, halved
½ c. butter, softened
2 tblsp. toasted sesame seeds

Place muffin halves on baking sheet. Lightly toast in 500° oven. Spread with softened butter and sprinkle with sesame seeds. Return to oven for 1 to 2 minutes. Serve at once. Makes 6 servings.

BAKED PEARS WITH MARSHMALLOW SAUCE

6 medium, firm-ripe Anjou or Bosc pears
¾ c. brown sugar, firmly packed
1½ c. water
1 tsp. grated lemon rind
1 tblsp. lemon juice
½ tsp. ground cloves
1½ tsp. warm water
1 c. marshmallow creme
2 tblsp. grated semi-sweet chocolate

Remove stems from pears. Pare strip about 2-inches wide from top of each pear. Place fruit upright in 8-inch square baking dish.

Combine brown sugar, 1½ c. water, lemon rind, lemon juice and cloves in small saucepan. Bring to boiling, stirring constantly. Pour hot syrup over pears.

Bake in 325° oven 1 to 1¼ hours or until tender, basting occasionally during baking. Serve in individual deep dishes.

Blend 1½ tsp. warm water into marshmallow creme. Spoon over warm baked pears and top with chocolate. Makes 6 servings.

MENU 2

Salmon Loaf with Swiss Cheese *
Crispy Potatoes *
Green Lima Beans *
Dilled Cucumber Pickles
Homemade Bread   Butter
Raspberry Sherbet
Beverage

* Recipes given

Shredded Swiss cheese is sprinkled over this flavorful salmon loaf for the last 5 minutes of baking time—makes a tasty easy topper. Corn flakes and butter give crispness to the potatoes.

SALMON LOAF WITH SWISS CHEESE

1 (1 lb.) can salmon
2 c. fresh bread crumbs
2 tsp. instant minced onion
1 tsp. dried parsley flakes
½ tsp. salt
⅛ tsp. pepper
Milk
1 egg, beaten
1 tsp. Worcestershire sauce
1 tblsp. lemon juice
2 tblsp. melted butter
⅓ c. shredded Swiss cheese

Drain salmon, reserving liquid. Flake salmon in mixing bowl. Add bread crumbs, onion, parsley flakes, salt and pepper.

19

Add enough milk to reserved salmon liquid to make ⅓ cup. Add ⅓ c. reserved liquid, egg, Worcestershire sauce and lemon juice to salmon mixture. Mix lightly and shape into loaf in greased 11x7x1½-inch baking dish.

Bake in 350° oven 40 minutes. Remove from oven. Brush top of loaf with melted butter and sprinkle with cheese. Return to oven and bake 5 more minutes. Makes 4 or 5 servings.

CRISPY POTATOES

4 or 5 medium potatoes, pared and quartered or 16 to 20 small new potatoes, pared
¼ c. melted butter
½ c. crushed corn flakes

Pat potatoes with paper towels to dry. Dip each in melted butter and roll into corn flakes. Arrange in greased shallow baking dish. Sprinkle with remaining crumbs.

Bake in 350° oven 55 minutes or until tender. (Drizzle with remaining melted butter once during baking.) Makes 4 or 5 servings.

GREEN LIMA BEANS

2 (1 lb. 1 oz.) cans green lima beans
Salt
Pepper
1 tblsp. butter

Drain beans, reserving 2 tblsp. liquid. Place beans and 2 tblsp. liquid in 1½-qt. casserole. Sprinkle with salt and pepper. Dot with butter. Cover.

Bake in 350° oven 20 to 25 minutes or until hot. Makes 4 or 5 servings.

MENU 3

Maple-Barbecued Chicken *
Baked Potatoes
Buttered Green Beans *
Assorted Crisp Relishes
Orange-Rhubarb Cobbler *
Beverage

* Recipes given

Prick potatoes with a fork and place in the oven with chicken. Add the beans and cobbler later. The combination of orange and rhubarb makes the dessert special.

MAPLE-BARBECUED CHICKEN

2 (2½ to 3 lb.) broiler-fryers, cut up
½ c. melted butter
2 small cloves garlic, minced
⅓ c. wine vinegar
2 tblsp. maple syrup
2 tsp. salt
⅛ tsp. pepper
½ tsp. dry mustard
½ tsp. marjoram leaves

Place chicken skin side down in large shallow baking pan. Combine butter, garlic, vinegar, maple syrup, salt, pepper, mustard and marjoram. Pour over chicken.

Bake in 425° oven 30 minutes. Turn chicken pieces. Baste with sauce and bake 30 more minutes or until chicken is tender. Makes 8 servings.

ORANGE-RHUBARB COBBLER

1¼ c. sugar
2 tblsp. cornstarch
½ tsp. ground nutmeg
½ c. orange juice
½ c. water
2 tblsp. butter
6 c. diced rhubarb, ¾-inch
2 c. unsifted flour
3 tsp. baking powder
1 tsp. salt
¼ c. sugar
½ c. flaked coconut
2 tsp. grated orange rind
¼ c. lard
2 tblsp. butter
1 c. milk

Combine 1¼ c. sugar, cornstarch and nutmeg in saucepan. Blend in orange juice and water. Cook over low heat, stirring constantly, until mixture boils and sugar is dissolved. Stir in 2 tblsp. butter and rhubarb; set aside.

Sift together flour, baking powder, salt and ¼ c. sugar into mixing bowl. Add coconut and orange rind. Cut in lard and 2 tblsp. butter with pastry blender or two knives until mixture resembles coarse meal. Quickly stir in milk to make soft dough.

Bring rhubarb mixture to boiling. Pour into 2½-qt.

baking dish. Spoon biscuit dough in 8 mounds on top of rhubarb.

Bake in 425° oven about 25 minutes or until biscuits are golden brown. Serve warm. Makes 8 servings.

BUTTERED GREEN BEANS

---

3 (10 oz.) pkgs. frozen cut green beans, thawed
1 tsp. salt
¼ c. butter

Place beans in 2-qt. casserole. Sprinkle with salt and dot with butter. Cover.

Bake in 425° oven 40 to 45 minutes or until tender. Stir after first 30 minutes of baking and again before serving. Makes 8 servings.

MENU 4

Roast Turkey Quarter *
Herb-seasoned Stuffing *
Baked Acorn Squash
Cranberry Sauce
Biscuits   Butter
Ice Cream
Beverage

*Recipes given

Allow about 1¼ hours of baking time for the acorn squash. Increase oven heat and bake the biscuits while the turkey is being carved and the rest of the food "dished up."

ROAST TURKEY QUARTER

1 (6 to 7 lb.) quarter roast of turkey
Salt
Cooking oil

Lightly season cut side of turkey roast with salt. Place, skin side up, on rack in shallow baking pan. Brush skin with cooking oil.

Roast in 325° oven 2½ to 3 hours or until meat thermometer registers 185°. Bake stuffing during the last hour of roasting time. Makes 6 to 8 servings.

HERB-SEASONED STUFFING

6 c. dry bread cubes (¼-inch)
½ tsp. salt
¾ tsp. thyme leaves
¾ tsp. rosemary leaves
2 tblsp. minced fresh parsley
1 tsp. instant chicken bouillon powder
2 tblsp. finely chopped onion
½ c. finely chopped celery
¼ c. butter
½ c. hot water (about)

Combine bread cubes, salt, thyme, rosemary, parsley and bouillon powder in large mixing bowl. Cook onion and celery in melted butter in small skillet until tender. Add to bread cubes. Add enough water to moisten, tossing lightly. Turn into 13x9x2-inch baking dish.

Bake in 325° oven 1 hour. Makes 6 servings.

MENU 5

Franks and Baked Potato Salad *
Caraway Coleslaw
Hot Rolls   Butter
Apple Crisp with Cheddar Cheese *
Beverage

* Recipes given

Bake your favorite yeast rolls ahead and freeze. Then just reheat. Your family will love the zippy flavor of this hot potato salad and the warm spicy apple crisp.

FRANKS AND BAKED POTATO SALAD

4 c. hot mashed potatoes
1 egg, slightly beaten
½ c. chopped celery
¼ c. finely chopped onion
¼ c. melted butter
1 tblsp. prepared mustard
2 tblsp. vinegar
Salt
Pepper
12 frankfurters

Beat together mashed potatoes and egg in large bowl. Add celery, onion, butter, mustard, vinegar, salt and pepper. Mix well. Turn into greased 9-inch square baking dish.

Bake in 350° oven 20 minutes. Top with frankfurters. Bake 20 more minutes. Makes 6 servings.

APPLE CRISP WITH CHEDDAR CHEESE

1 (1 lb. 4 oz.) can pie-sliced apples,
    drained
1 tsp. grated lemon rind
1 tblsp. lemon juice
¼ c. flour
1 c. quick-cooking rolled oats
½ c. brown sugar, firmly packed
½ tsp. salt
1 tsp. ground cinnamon
½ c. melted butter
½ c. shredded Cheddar cheese

Place apples in buttered 9-inch round cake dish. Sprinkle with lemon rind and juice.

Combine flour, oats, brown sugar, salt, cinnamon and melted butter in bowl. Stir with fork until mixture is crumbly. Sprinkle over apples.

Bake in 350° oven about 40 minutes or until apples are tender. Remove from oven and sprinkle with cheese. Serve warm. Makes 6 servings.

MENU 6

Hawaiian Ham Slices *
Buttered Sweet Potatoes
Broccoli Custard *
Hot Rolls   Butter
Oven-toasted Pound Cake
Berry Sauce
Beverage

* Recipes given

Heat canned or cooked fresh sweet potatoes in a baking dish along with the ham and broccoli custard. Then increase the temperature and oven-toast slices of your favorite pound cake. Serve with a fresh berry sauce.

HAWAIIAN HAM SLICES

> **1 (15¼ oz.) can sliced pineapple**
> **1 tblsp. soy sauce**
> **1 tsp. ground ginger**
> **1 small clove garlic, minced**
> **8 serving-size slices fully-cooked ham,**
>   **about ½-inch thick**

Drain pineapple, reserving juice. Combine juice, soy sauce, ginger and garlic; mix well. Pour over ham slices in shallow baking dish. Cover and refrigerate at least 2 to 3 hours. Turn slices once about halfway through marinating time.

Remove ham slices from marinade and place in greased 13x9x2-inch baking dish.

Bake in 350° oven 15 minutes. Turn ham slices, place a pineapple ring on each and brush meat and pineapple with marinade. Return to oven and bake 15 more minutes. Makes 8 servings.

BROCCOLI CUSTARD

---

1 tblsp. instant minced onion
¼ c. butter
¼ c. flour
1½ tsp. salt
⅛ tsp. pepper
1 tsp. Worcestershire sauce
1½ c. milk
2 (10 oz.) pkgs. frozen chopped broccoli, thawed
3 eggs, slightly beaten

Saute onion in melted butter in skillet until golden. Blend in flour, salt, pepper and Worcestershire sauce. Gradually stir in milk. Cook over medium heat, stirring constantly, until mixture is thickened. Add broccoli. Continue cooking until well heated.

Blend a little of broccoli mixture into eggs; mix well. Return egg mixture to saucepan, stirring well. Pour into greased 1½-qt. casserole.

Bake in 350° oven 45 to 50 minutes or until knife inserted halfway between edge of dish and center comes out clean. Makes 8 servings.

CHAPTER III

Company Fare

Oven meals can be simple and substantial or they can be quite elegant meals you proudly serve to company or to the family on special-occasion days.

Start with the main course and let its baking temperature and time set the pace for the other foods you choose. Select an outstanding dish that's exceptionally good eating and that looks as good as it tastes—one that you know will bring rave compliments.

Ovenproof platters and well-designed casseroles which can travel from oven to table really make an oven meal look handsome. Attractive individual casseroles or shallow bakers not only simplify serving but add a distinctive touch to the meal.

Instead of using a rectangular pan for baking a loaf mixture, why not try a large ring mold? Fill the center with a bright-colored vegetable, which has been baked in the oven. Or, bake the mixture in a round cake dish and cut wedges for a change of pace.

Plan a potato, rice, pasta or other accompaniment that's a little more dressed up than for everyday— maybe Potato Puffs, Poppy Seed Noodles or Cheddar Cheese and Rice Ring (see recipes). Give vegetables a new look with a different seasoning or sauce; or combine several vegetables in a casserole and top with buttered crumbs.

Dramatize the meal with hot bread and a luscious frozen dessert, both of which could be make-aheads and come from the freezer.

Colorful garnishes can make a meal look beautiful—

29

try chilled cherry tomatoes, spiced fruit, parsley or watercress. But, hot garnishes which can bake right along with the other food are easy and unusual. Try baking thick orange slices, lightly curried grapefruit sections, peach halves, pineapple rings or apple slices just brushed with butter and drizzled with maple syrup or honey to give a shiny glaze. They'll add a special touch to your company meals.

MENU 1

Currant-Glazed Ham Slice *
Escalloped Potatoes
Butternut Squash Bake *
Apple Pineapple Salad
Hot Rolls   Butter
Tart Shells *
with Assorted Ice Creams
and Toppings
Beverage

*Recipes given

Heat frozen tart shells (see Index for recipe) in the oven before you bake this bound-to-please company meal. Let the freezer provide the rolls, too, to heat just before dinner is served.

CURRANT-GLAZED HAM SLICE

1 (2½ to 3 lb.) center-cut ham slice,
  1½-inches thick
¼ c. red currant jelly
1 tblsp. light corn syrup
½ tsp. grated lemon rind
10 to 12 whole cloves

Slash fat edge of ham slice at 1-inch intervals. Place in shallow baking dish. Cover with aluminum foil. Bake in 325° oven 50 minutes.

Combine jelly, corn syrup and lemon rind in saucepan. Heat, stirring constantly, until blended.

Remove ham from oven. Stud outer edge of fat with cloves and spoon half of glaze over ham. Return to oven, uncovered, for 10 minutes. Spoon on remaining glaze and bake 10 more minutes. Makes 6 servings.

BUTTERNUT SQUASH BAKE

5 to 6 lb. butternut squash, unpared
½ tsp. salt
⅛ tsp. pepper
3 tblsp. butter
½ c. water
½ c. walnut halves

Cut butternut squash in crosswise slices, about ½-inch thick. Arrange slices in shallow baking dish, overlapping each. Sprinkle with salt and pepper; dot with butter. Add water. Cover.

Bake in 325° oven about 1 hour. Remove from oven. Top with walnut halves. Return to oven, uncovered, for 10 more minutes. Makes 6 servings.

ASSORTED ICE CREAM TARTS

---

6 frozen tart shells (see Index)
Assorted ice creams
Assorted toppings (fruit, sauce, nuts,
whipped cream, etc.)

Place frozen tart shells on baking sheet.

Heat in 325° oven 6 to 8 minutes. Cool on rack.

At serving time, fill with ice cream and top as desired. Makes 6 servings.

MENU 2

Roast Ducklings
with Orange-Pecan Stuffing *
Potato Puffs*
Buttered Asparagus
Bibb Lettuce with French Dressing
Dinner Rolls   Butter
Hot Fruit Compote *
Cookies
Beverage

* Recipes given

Twin ducklings lend a festive note to this dinner as does the elegant fruit compote that bakes along with them for part of the time. Potato Puffs are heated in a 500° oven while the ducks are being carved.

ROAST DUCKLINGS WITH ORANGE-PECAN STUFFING

¼ c. chopped onion
1 c. coarsely chopped pecans
½ c. butter
8 c. toasted bread cubes
½ tsp. salt
¼ tsp. pepper
1½ tsp. poultry seasoning
2 tsp. grated orange rind
½ c. orange juice (about)
2 (4 to 5 lb.) Long Island ducklings
Salt

Cook onion and pecans in melted butter in skillet until onion is tender. Combine bread cubes, salt, pepper, poultry seasoning and orange rind in mixing bowl. Add onion mixture. Toss together lightly, adding enough orange juice to moisten.

Lightly season cavities of ducklings with salt. Stuff with bread mixture and truss. Prick skin all over with tines of fork. Place ducklings on rack in shallow roasting pan.

Bake in 325° oven 2½ to 2¾ hours or until tender. Garnish with orange wedges and curly endive if you wish. Makes 8 servings.

POTATO PUFFS

4 c. hot mashed potatoes
2 tblsp. melted butter
1 egg, slightly beaten
½ tsp. salt
⅛ tsp. pepper
2 tblsp. butter
2 tblsp. chopped pimientos

Combine mashed potatoes, 2 tblsp. butter, egg, salt and pepper in bowl; mix well. Shape mixture into 8 mounds on greased baking sheet, about ½ c. each. Make a slight indentation in center of each with spoon. Dot with 2 tblsp. butter. Garnish with pimientos.

Bake in 500° oven 10 minutes or until lightly browned. Makes 8 servings.

HOT FRUIT COMPOTE

1 (1 lb. 6 oz.) can peach pie filling
1 (1 lb. 4 oz.) can pineapple chunks in
    pineapple juice
1 (1 lb.) can sliced pears, drained
1 (1 lb.) can pitted dark sweet cherries,
    drained
1 tblsp. grated lemon rind
2 tblsp. lemon juice
1 tsp. ground nutmeg
1 c . dairy sour cream

Combine pie filling, undrained pineapple, pears and cherries in 2-qt. casserole. Gently stir in lemon rind, lemon juice and nutmeg. Cover.

Heat in 325° oven about 40 minutes. Serve warm in individual dessert dishes with a dollop of sour cream. Makes 8 servings.

MENU 3

Cheddar Cheese and Rice Ring *
Buttered Peas and Mushrooms *
Chilled Tomato Wedges
Little Crusty Rolls *   **Butter**
Almond Toffee Cake *
Beverage

* Recipes given

Ideal menu for a luncheon or brunch. Do the rolls ahead and freeze, then heat at serving time and bring them to the table hot and crusty. Freeze the Almond Toffee Cake ahead (see Index for recipe).

BUTTERED PEAS AND MUSHROOMS

---

2 (10 oz.) pkgs. frozen peas, thawed
1 (4 oz.) can mushrooms, drained
¾ tsp. salt
¼ c. butter

Place peas and mushrooms in 1½-qt. casserole Sprinkle with salt and dot with butter. Cover.

Bake in 375° oven 45 to 50 minutes or until tender.

Stir after first half hour of baking and again before serving. Makes 8 servings.

LITTLE CRUSTY ROLLS

1 pkg. active dry yeast
¼ c. warm water (110-115°)
¾ c. boiling water
1 tblsp. sugar
1½ tsp. salt
2 tblsp. shortening
3 to 3½ c. unsifted flour
2 egg whites, stiffly beaten
1 egg white
1 tblsp. water

Sprinkle yeast on warm water; stir to dissolve.

Combine boiling water, sugar, salt and shortening in mixing bowl. Cool to lukewarm.

Add 1 c. flour and yeast mixture to milk mixture; beat well. Fold in stiffly beaten egg whites. Beat in enough remaining flour to make a soft dough. Knead on floured surface until smooth and elastic, about 10 minutes. Place in lightly oiled bowl, turning dough to oil top. Cover and let rise in warm place until doubled.

Punch down. Divide dough in half. Shape each into 12 round or oval rolls. Place rolls, 2½-inches apart, on greased baking sheet. Cover and let rise until doubled, about 45 minutes. Brush with the remaining egg white beaten with the 1 tblsp. water. Place large shallow pan of hot water on bottom rack of oven to give rolls crispness.

Bake in 450° oven 12 to 15 minutes or until golden brown. Makes 2 dozen rolls.

CHEDDAR CHEESE AND RICE RING

1¾ c. milk
¼ c. butter
1 c. fresh bread crumbs
2 c. cooked rice
1 tblsp. chopped onion
1 tsp. salt
3 c. shredded sharp Cheddar cheese
3 eggs, beaten
1 tsp. Worcestershire sauce
Buttered Peas and Mushrooms
    (see recipe)
Tomato wedges
Parsley

Scald milk with butter in saucepan. Combine bread crumbs, rice, onion, salt, cheese, eggs and Worcestershire sauce in bowl. Pour hot milk mixture overall; blend thoroughly. Turn into well-buttered 6-cup ring mold set in pan of hot water.

Bake in 375° oven 55 to 60 minutes or until delicately browned. Turn out onto large chop plate and fill center with Buttered Peas and Mushrooms. Garnish with tomato wedges and parsley. Makes 8 servings.

MENU 4

Roast Whole Beef Tenderloin *
Special Stuffed Baked Potatoes *
Herbed Frenched Green Beans *
Avocado-Grapefruit Salad
Hot Garlic Bread
Pineapple Cheesecake*
Beverage

*Recipes given

You'll win an award for this dinner! The touch of herbs in the Frenched green beans compliment the flavor of the tender, juicy beef. Put the garlic bread in the oven just before serving, to have it piping hot and fragrant. (See Index for Pineapple Cheesecake recipe.)

ROAST WHOLE BEEF TENDERLOIN

---

1 (4 to 6 lb.) whole beef tenderloin
Cooking oil
Garlic salt
Pepper

Trim excess surface fat and connective tissue from meat. Place meat on rack in shallow baking pan, tucking small end under to make roast of uniform size. Brush with cooking oil and season with garlic salt and pepper.

Roast in 425° oven 45 minutes to 1 hour or until meat thermometer registers 140°. Carve crosswise in 1-inch slices to serve. Makes 8 servings.

SPECIAL STUFFED BAKED POTATOES

**8 medium baking potatoes
1 c. light cream
¼ c. butter
1 tsp. salt
⅛ tsp. pepper
3 strips bacon, cooked, drained and
    crumbled**

Bake potatoes in 425° oven 1 hour or until tender. Cut lengthwise slice from top of each and scoop out potato. Place potatoes in bowl. Mash well. Add cream, butter, salt and pepper; beat until fluffy. Lightly pile mixture into potato shells on baking pan and sprinkle crumbled bacon on top. Return to oven.

Bake in 425° oven 5 more minutes or until thoroughly heated. Makes 8 servings.

HERBED FRENCHED GREEN BEANS

**3 (9 oz.) pkgs. frozen French-style
    green beans, partially thawed
¾ tsp. salt
½ tsp. rosemary leaves
1 tblsp. water
2 tblsp. butter**

Place beans in 2-qt. casserole. Add salt, rosemary and water. Dot with butter. Cover.

Bake in 425° oven 35 to 40 minutes. Stir after the

first 15 minutes of baking and again before serving. Makes 8 servings.

MENU 5

Baked Center-cut Pork Chops *
with Glazed Apple Rings *
Corn Pudding *
Tossed Green Salad
Dilled French Bread *
Pineapple Upside-down Cake
Beverage

* Recipes given

Individual portions of meat, like pork chops, simplify serving, especially when the glazed apple garnish is "attached." Corn pudding is a pleasant change of pace from potatoes.

BAKED CENTER-CUT PORK CHOPS

6 center-cut pork chops, 1-inch thick
Salt
Pepper
2 large red apples
1 tblsp. lemon juice
2 tblsp. brown sugar, firmly packed

Season pork chops with salt and pepper. Arrange chops, about 2-inches apart, in large shallow baking pan.

Bake in 350° oven 1¼ hours.

Core apples, but do not pare. Cut in ½-inch slices. Place an apple slice on each chop. Brush apple with lemon juice and sprinkle with brown sugar. Cover loosely with aluminum foil.

Bake 15 more minutes or until chops are tender. Makes 6 servings.

CORN PUDDING

1 (1 lb.) can whole kernel corn, drained (2 c.)
¼ c. finely chopped onion
3 eggs, slightly beaten
2 tblsp. flour
2 tsp. sugar
2 tblsp. melted butter
1½ c. milk
1 tsp. salt
⅛ tsp. pepper

Combine corn, onion and eggs in bowl. Blend in flour, sugar, butter, milk, salt and pepper. Pour into greased 1-qt. casserole. Set in pan of hot water.

Bake in 350° oven about 1 hour and 20 minutes or until firm. Makes 6 servings.

DILLED FRENCH BREAD

1 (1 lb.) loaf French bread
½ c. butter, softened
2 tblsp. dill weed

Cut loaf in diagonal ¾-inch slices, cutting to within ¼-inch of bottom crust. Blend together butter and dill weed. Spread butter mixture one side of each slice of bread. Wrap bread in aluminum foil.

Heat in 350° oven about 15 minutes or until hot. Makes 6 servings.

MENU 6

Beef Roll-ups *
Poppy Seed Noodles *
Baked Onion Halves *
Molded Vegetable Salad
Rolls   Butter
Lemon Sherbet   Butter Cookies
Beverage

* Recipes given

The poppy seed noodles and the onions bake in less time than the "rouladens," as these flavorful meat rolls are called in Germany. So, schedule your meal accordingly.

BAKED ONION HALVES

4 medium sweet onions
Salt
Pepper
2 tblsp. butter
2 tblsp. water
¼ c. shredded sharp Cheddar cheese
¼ c. dry bread crumbs
1 tblsp. melted butter

Peel onions and cut in half crosswise. Place in shallow baking dish. Sprinkle lightly with salt and pepper. Dot with 2 tblsp. butter. Add water. Cover.

Bake in 350° oven about 1 hour or until almost tender. Combine cheese, bread crumbs and melted butter. Spoon on top of onions.

Bake, uncovered, 15 more minutes or until cheese is melted and crumbs are brown. Makes 8 servings.

BEEF ROLL-UPS

2½ lbs. round steak, ¼-inch thick
¼ c. finely chopped celery
¼ c. prepared mustard
4 strips bacon, cut in half
1 large dill pickle, cut in 8 strips
2 tblsp. flour
1½ tsp. salt
⅛ tsp. pepper
3 tblsp. cooking oil
1 (8 oz.) can tomato sauce
1 tsp. Worcestershire sauce
1 tsp. instant beef bouillon powder
1 c. hot water
Poppy Seed Noodles (recipe follows)

Pound steak with meat mallet to flatten slightly. Trim off excess fat. Cut meat in 8 pieces about 2½x4½ inches. Combine celery and mustard in small bowl. Spread mustard mixture on meat to about ½-inch from edges. Top with half strips of bacon and pickle. Roll up each piece like a jelly roll and tie securely near both ends with cord. Coat in mixture of flour, salt and pepper. Brown slowly and evenly in hot oil in skillet. Transfer to 13x9x2-inch baking dish.

Pour off excess fat from skillet. Stir in tomato sauce, Worcestershire sauce, beef bouillon powder and water. Bring to a boil. Pour over meat rolls. Cover.

Bake in 350° oven about 1½ hours or until tender. Thicken sauce with flour-water paste, if you wish. Serve over Poppy Seed Noodles. Makes 8 servings.

POPPY SEED NOODLES

---

12 oz. medium noodles
1½ tsp. salt
¼ c. butter
6 c. boiling water
1 tblsp. poppy seed

Spread noodles in 15x10¼x2¼-inch baking pan. Add salt, butter and water; stir well. Cover.

Bake in 350° oven 35 to 40 minutes or until tender, but still firm. Stir in poppy seeds. Makes 8 servings.

MENU 7

Baked Stuffed Ham *
Golden Potato Squares *
Tangy Cabbage Slaw
Cheese Crescents *   **Butter**
Individual Schaum Tortes *
Coffee   Milk

* Recipes given

Easy-to-prepare Easter dinner for 12 guests. The Cheese Crescents can be baked ahead and frozen. Then just reheat when ham is removed from the oven.

GOLDEN POTATO SQUARES

5 lbs. potatoes
1½ c. chopped onion
⅔ c. butter
1 (13 oz.) can evaporated milk
4 eggs, beaten
2½ tsp. salt
¼ tsp. pepper
¼ c. minced fresh parsley
1½ c. shredded Cheddar cheese

Pare potatoes and place immediately in a large bowl with enough cold water to cover.

Saute onion in melted butter in skillet until tender. Add evaporated milk; bring to a boil. Remove from heat; set aside.

Combine eggs, salt and pepper in large glass bowl; beat until frothy. Shred potatoes using medium blade of shredder. Place immediately into egg mixture, turning to coat well. (This helps prevent discoloration of potatoes.) Add parsley, 1 c. cheese and milk mixture; mix well. Turn into greased 13x9x2-inch baking dish.

Bake in 350° oven 1 hour. Top with remaining ½ c. cheese. Bake 30 more minutes or until potatoes are done. Cut in squares. Makes 12 servings.

BAKED STUFFED HAM

1 (5 lb.) canned ham
¾ c. chopped onion
¾ c. chopped celery
6 tblsp. butter
4½ c. fresh bread cubes (¼ inch)
1½ c. chopped pared apples
⅓ c. raisins
1 c. chicken broth
2 tblsp. minced fresh parsley
½ tsp. ground cinnamon
1 (10 oz.) jar pineapple preserves

Cut ham into 20 (⅜-inch) slices using electric or sharp kitchen knife. Place in aluminum foil-lined jelly roll pan or shallow roasting pan.

Saute onion and celery in melted butter in skillet until tender. Combine bread cubes, apples, raisins, chicken broth, parsley, cinnamon and sauteed vegetables in large bowl. Mix lightly, but well.

Arrange stuffing between slices, leaving 2 slices between stuffing layers. Tie securely with string. Cover loosely with aluminum foil.

Bake in 350° oven 1 hour.

Meanwhile, melt preserves in small saucepan over low heat, stirring occasionally.

Remove aluminum foil. Continue baking 1 more hour, basting with preserves several times the last 30 minutes. Bake until stuffing registers 165° on meat thermometer. Remove from oven. Let stand 10 minutes. Makes 12 servings.

CHEESE CRESCENTS

2 c. sifted flour
3 tsp. baking powder
1 tsp. salt
½ c. shortening
¾ c. milk
1 tblsp. melted butter
2 tblsp. grated Parmesan cheese
1 tblsp. minced fresh parsley
Milk

Sift together flour, baking powder and salt into bowl. Cut in shortening until mixture resembles coarse crumbs. Add ¾ c. milk; mix well. Place dough on floured surface.

Knead lightly 10 times. Roll into 13-inch circle. Brush with melted butter. Sprinkle with Parmesan cheese and parsley. Cut into 12 wedges. Roll up each from wide end. Place crescents, point down, on greased baking sheet. Brush with milk.

Bake in 425° oven 25 minutes or until golden brown. Makes 12.

INDIVIDUAL SCHAUM TORTES

8 egg whites
½ tsp. cream of tartar
2 c. sugar
1 tsp. vanilla
1 tsp. vinegar
2 qts. fresh strawberries, sliced
and sweetened or 3 (10 oz.)
pkgs. frozen strawberries, thawed
2 c. heavy cream, whipped and
sweetened

Beat egg whites in large bowl with electric mixer at high speed until frothy. Add cream of tartar; beat until egg whites are almost dry.

Slowly add sugar, 2 tblsp. at a time, beating well after each addition. (Total beating time: 20 minutes.) Add vanilla and vinegar; beat 2 minutes. (Mixture should be very stiff and glossy.) Drop mixture by spoonfuls onto greased baking sheets, making 12 tortes.

Bake in 250° oven 1 hour 15 minutes or until pale brown and crusty. Remove from baking sheets; cool on racks. Schaum Tortes can be stored in covered container up to 1 month.

To serve: Spoon strawberries over each torte and top with whipped cream. Makes 12 servings.

CHAPTER IV

Roasts
with Extra Dividends

The double batch or "cook once for twice" practice is a great way to save time and energy and stock up for periods when you're too busy to cook.

The time required for roasting a large cut of meat or a hefty turkey is really not too much longer than that required for a small cut.

For example, a 12 to 14 lb. bone-in whole ham, labeled fully cooked, takes about 2¾ to 3 hours to heat, while a fully cooked half ham, 6 to 7 lbs., takes 2 to 2¼ hours. A 12 lb. turkey, stuffed, roasts in 4½ hours, only half again as long as is required for a 6 lb. bird. So you save time and oven heat. Also, the larger ham or turkey will yield more meat in proportion to bone, so you'll save money as well.

The versatility of this dividend roast meat or poultry makes it especially appealing to busy homemakers. You can create a great variety of dishes from whole slices of meat to the tag ends and bones for a nourishing soup base. Small leftover pieces can be ground or chopped.

For convenience, if you're not using the meat or poultry within a few days, freeze it in the amounts and in the form you're apt to use it. Remember that slices and pieces will keep best when protected by broth, gravy or sauce. If you don't have regular broth on hand, you'll find the instant bouillon powder or bouillon cubes convenient.

Remember, too, to use those packages while the contents are still top quality—large pieces of meat or poultry, well-wrapped, within a month or two; the slices or smaller pieces, within 2 to 4 months.

CORNED BEEF BRISKET OR ROUND

**2 (3 to 4 lb.) corned beef briskets or
rounds for oven roasting**

Place corned beef, fat side up, on rack in large shallow baking pan. Do not cover.

Roast in 325° oven about 3 hours or until tender. If you wish, sprinkle brown sugar over top of meat during the last 15 minutes of roasting time.

One brisket or round makes about 6 dinner servings. Refrigerate or freeze the other for later use.

BAKE-ALONG IDEA: Scalloped Potatoes Supreme *
DIVIDEND IDEAS: Baked Reuben Fondue *
                        Corned Beef Pinwheels *
* Recipes given   Corned Beef-Macaroni Salad *

SCALLOPED POTATOES SUPREME

**4 c. thinly sliced, pared potatoes
(about 6 medium)
¾ c. coarsely chopped onion
1 (10½ oz.) can condensed cream
of celery soup
¼ c. milk
¼ tsp. salt
⅛ tsp. pepper
1 c. shredded Cheddar cheese
Paprika**

Combine potatoes and onion in 2-qt. casserole. Mix together soup, milk, salt and pepper in bowl. Pour over potato mixture. Cover.

Bake in 325° oven 1 hour.

Uncover and top with cheese. Sprinkle with paprika. Continue baking 30 more minutes or until potatoes are tender and top is golden brown. Makes 6 servings.

BAKED REUBEN FONDUE

---

6 slices rye bread, cut in cubes
2 tsp. dried parsley flakes
2 c. shaved cooked corned beef
½ c. chopped onion
¼ c. chopped celery
¾ tsp. salt
⅛ tsp. pepper
1 tsp. dry mustard
½ c. mayonnaise
1 c. drained sauerkraut
4 eggs, slightly beaten
2½ c. milk
½ c. shredded Swiss cheese

Arrange bread cubes on baking sheet. Toast lightly in oven. Combine with parsley flakes. Place half of mixture in bottom of greased 8- or 9-inch square baking pan. Combine corned beef, onion, celery, salt, pepper, mustard and mayonnaise in bowl. Spoon over bread cubes. Top with sauerkraut and remaining bread cubes.

Blend eggs and milk in bowl; pour over all. Cover and chill at least an hour or overnight.

Bake, uncovered, in 325° oven 55 minutes or until set. Sprinkle cheese over top and return to oven a few more minutes to melt cheese. Let stand about 5 minutes before cutting in squares. Makes 9 servings.

CORNED BEEF PINWHEELS

2½ c. ground or finely chopped cooked
   corned beef
2 tblsp. finely chopped onion
¼ c. mayonnaise
2 tblsp. prepared mustard
1 tsp. Worcestershire sauce
Biscuit Dough (using 2 c. flour)

Combine corned beef, onion, mayonnaise, mustard and Worcestershire sauce in bowl.

Prepare your favorite biscuit dough and roll out on floured surface to 12x8-inch rectangle. Spread meat mixture over surface of dough almost to edges and roll from long side, jelly roll fashion. Pinch edges to seal. Cut in 12 (1-inch) slices and place, cut side down, on lightly greased baking sheet.

Bake in 425° oven 15 minutes or until lightly browned. Serve with horseradish-spiked cream sauce or with a creamed green vegetable. Makes 6 servings.

CORNED BEEF-MACARONI SALAD

2 c. cubed cooked corned beef
1 (8 oz.) pkg. shell macaroni,
    cooked and drained
1 c. sliced celery
¼ c. chopped green onions
¼ c. pickle relish
2 tsp. prepared mustard
½ c. mayonnaise

Combine corned beef, macaroni, celery, green onions and pickle relish in large bowl. Blend mustard and mayonnaise in another bowl. Add to corned beef mixture and toss lightly until all ingredients are coated with dressing. Chill well. Makes 6 servings.

BAKED HAM

Select ham of desired weight and bake in 325° oven for following approximate times:

FULLY COOKED HAMS:

Bone-in Whole Hams	8-10 lbs.	2¼ to 2½ hours
	12-14 lbs.	2¾ to 3 hours
	16-18 lbs.	3¼ to 3½ hours
Bone-in Half Ham	6-8 lbs.	2 to 2¼ hours
Boneless Whole Ham	8-10 lbs.	2 to 2¼ hours
Boneless Half Ham	4-5 lbs.	1½ hours

COOK BEFORE EATING HAMS:

Bone-in Whole Hams	8-10 lbs.	2¾ to 3 hours
	12-14 lbs.	3¼ to 3½ hours
	16-18 lbs.	3¾ to 4 hours
Bone-in Half Ham	6-8 lbs.	2 to 2½ hours

CANNED HAMS:

	3-5 lbs.	1¼ to 1½ hours
	6-6¾ lbs.	1¾ to 2 hours
	9-10 lbs.	2¼ to 2¾ hours
	10-12 lbs.	2¾ to 3 hours
	13 lbs.	3½ hours

BAKE-ALONG IDEAS: Colcannon *
Scalloped Apples or Pears
Baked Apples or Pears

DIVIDEND IDEAS: Ham and Cabbage Soup *
Ham Patties with Tangy Meat Sauce *
Ham and Blue Cheese Open-Facers *

* Recipes given

COLCANNON

**6 medium potatoes, pared and quartered
(about 2 lbs.)
1 tsp. salt
4 c. shredded cabbage
½ tsp. salt
⅓ c. milk
¼ c. soft butter
½ c. thinly sliced green onions
⅛ tsp. pepper
2 tblsp. butter**

Add potatoes and 1 tsp. salt to 2-inches boiling water in medium saucepan. Cover and bring back to a boil. Reduce heat and simmer until tender, about 30 minutes. Drain well. Gently shake potatoes in saucepan over low heat to dry.

Meanwhile, add cabbage and ½ tsp. salt to 1-inch boiling water in another saucepan. Cover and bring back to a boil. Reduce heat and simmer until tender, about 5 minutes. Drain well.

Mash potatoes with a vegetable masher until free of lumps. Add milk, a little at a time, beating well after each addition. Add ¼ c. butter. Beat with vegetable masher until potatoes are light and fluffy. Stir in drained cabbage, green onions and pepper. Turn into greased 1½-qt. casserole. Dot with 2 tblsp. butter.

Bake in 325° oven until hot. Makes 8 servings.

HAM AND CABBAGE SOUP

¼ c. chopped onion
¼ c. chopped celery
2 tblsp. butter
¼ c. flour
½ tsp. salt
⅛ tsp. pepper
3 c. hot water
2 c. shredded cabbage
1 bay leaf
2 c. diced cooked ham
¾ c. dairy sour cream
2 tblsp. chopped fresh parsley

Cook celery and onion in melted butter in Dutch oven until onion is tender. Blend in flour, salt and pepper. Stir in water and cook, stirring constantly, until mixture is boiling. Add cabbage and bay leaf; cover. Simmer 8 to 10 minutes or until cabbage is tender. Remove bay leaf. Stir in ham and cook 3 to 4 more minutes. Gently blend in sour cream. Heat a few more minutes. Do not boil. Garnish with parsley. Makes 6 servings.

HAM PATTIES WITH TANGY MEAT SAUCE

3 c. ground cooked ham
1 tblsp. chopped green onions
½ c. fresh bread crumbs
¼ c. milk
1 egg, slightly beaten
⅛ tsp. pepper
2 tblsp. cooking oil
1 tblsp. butter
1 tblsp. flour
¼ tsp. salt
1 tblsp. sugar
1½ tsp. prepared mustard
½ tsp. Worcestershire sauce
2 egg yolks, slightly beaten
½ c. pineapple juice
½ c. light cream
3 tblsp. prepared horseradish

Combine ham, green onions, bread crumbs, milk, 1 egg and pepper in bowl; mix lightly. Shape into 6 patties and brown slowly on both sides in hot cooking oil in heavy skillet.

Melt butter in heavy saucepan. Blend in flour, salt, sugar, mustard and Worcestershire sauce. Blend together egg yolks and pineapple juice; stir into first mixture. Blend in cream and cook over low heat, stirring constantly, until mixture is bubbling and thickened. Blend in horseradish. Serve hot over Ham Patties. Makes about 2 c. sauce. (Sauce is delicious served well chilled with cold baked ham.) Makes 6 servings.

HAM AND BLUE CHEESE OPEN-FACERS

4 slices toast
Butter
2 c. shredded lettuce
8 thin slices cooked ham
2 tblsp. chili sauce
1 c. mayonnaise
½ c. crumbled blue cheese

Spread toast with butter and top each slice with shredded lettuce. Overlap ham slices on lettuce. Blend chili sauce and mayonnaise in small bowl. Gently stir in the crumbled cheese. Spoon dressing over ham. Garnish sandwiches with crisp relishes and black olives if you wish. Makes 4 servings.

ROAST TURKEY

Select turkey of desired weight and stuff if you wish. Roast in 325° oven for following approximate times or until thermometer inserted in thigh registers 180 to 185°. (If you wish, roast turkey unstuffed and reduce roasting time by about ½ hour.)

Ready-to-Cook Weight	Approximate Roasting Time
6 lbs.	3 hours
8 lbs.	3½ hours
12 lbs.	4½ hours
16 lbs.	5½ hours
20 lbs.	6¼ hours

BAKE-ALONG IDEA: Cranberry Orange Upside-down Cake *

DIVIDEND IDEAS: Hot Turkey Salad *
                     Turkey-Broccoli Casserole *
                     Baked Turkey Squares *

* Recipes given

HOT TURKEY SALAD

---

    4 c. cubed cooked turkey
    1½ c. chopped celery
    ½ c. finely chopped green pepper
    2 tblsp. minced onion
    1 c. mayonnaise
    2 tblsp. lemon juice
    1 tsp. prepared mustard
    1 tsp. salt
    ⅛ tsp. pepper
    1 c. shredded Cheddar cheese
    1 c. crushed potato chips

Combine turkey, celery, green pepper and onion in mixing bowl. Blend together mayonnaise, lemon juice, mustard, salt and pepper in small bowl. Add to turkey mixture; toss lightly. Spoon mixture into 2-qt. shallow baking dish or 6 shallow individual casseroles. Top with Cheddar cheese and potato chips.

Bake in 350° oven 25 to 30 minutes or until thoroughly heated. Makes 6 servings.

TURKEY-BROCCOLI CASSEROLE

¼ c. butter
¼ c. flour
1 tsp. salt
⅛ tsp. pepper
2 c. chicken broth or milk
1 c . shredded sharp aged Cheddar cheese
2 (10 oz.) pkgs. frozen broccoli spears, cooked and drained
2½ c. sliced cooked turkey
Paprika

Melt butter in 2-qt. saucepan. Blend in flour, salt and pepper to make a smooth paste. Stir in broth. Cook over low heat, stirring constantly, until sauce is bubbling and thickened. Add cheese and stir until melted. Remove from heat.

Arrange broccoli in bottom of greased 11x7x1½-inch baking dish. Arrange turkey slices on top, overlapping slightly. Pour cheese sauce overall.

Bake in 400° oven 15 to 20 minutes. Sprinkle paprika on top. Makes 6 servings.

CRANBERRY ORANGE UPSIDE-DOWN CAKE

2 tblsp. melted butter
1 c. brown sugar, firmly packed
2 oranges, peeled and sliced
2 c. raw cranberries
½ c. butter
1½ c. sugar
2 eggs
2 c. sifted flour
1 tsp. baking powder
½ tsp. baking soda
½ tsp. salt
½ c. milk
½ c. orange juice
2 tsp. grated orange rind

Drizzle 2 tblsp. melted butter over bottom of 13x9x2-inch baking pan and sprinkle brown sugar evenly over butter. Cut orange slices in half and arrange in rows over sugar. Add cranberries, distributing evenly.

Cream together ½ c. butter and sugar in bowl until light and fluffy. Beat in eggs.

Sift together flour, baking powder, baking soda and salt. Add to creamed mixture alternately with milk and orange juice. Stir in orange rind. Pour over first layer in pan.

Bake in 350° oven 45 to 50 minutes. Turn out at once onto platter. Serve warm or cool. Makes 16 servings.

BAKED TURKEY SQUARES

3 c. cubed cooked turkey
2½ c. soft bread crumbs
1 tsp. salt
⅛ tsp. pepper
2 tblsp. chopped pimientos
2 c. turkey broth or milk
   (or 2 chicken bouillon cubes dissolved
   in 2 c. hot water and slightly cooled)
3 eggs, slightly beaten
Buttered crumbs

Combine turkey, bread crumbs, salt, pepper and pimientos in bowl. Spoon into greased 9-inch square baking dish. Blend broth into eggs in bowl. Pour over turkey mixture. Wreathe with buttered crumbs.

Bake in 350° oven 45 to 50 minutes or until knife inserted halfway between center and edge of mixture comes out clean. Cut in squares. Makes 9 servings.

ROAST BEEF

Select preferred cut of beef for roasting. Do not cover. Roast in 325° oven (unless otherwise specified) for following approximate times or to desired internal degree of doneness.

Cut and Weight	Internal Temp. on Removal from Oven	Approximate Cooking Time
Standing Rib, 4 to 6 lbs.	140° (rare)	2¼ to 2¾ hours
	160° (medium)	2¾ to 3¼ hours
	170° (well-done)	3¼ to 3½ hours
Standing Rib 6 to 8 lbs.	140°	2¾ to 3 hours
	160°	3 to 3½ hours
	170°	3¾ to 4 hours
Rolled Rib, 5 to 7 lbs.	140°	3¼ to 3½ hours
	160°	3¾ to 4 hours
	170°	4½ to 4¾ hours
Rolled Rump, 4 to 6 lbs.	150° to 170°	2 to 2½ hours
Sirloin Tip, 3½ to 4 lbs.	150° to 170°	2 to 2¾ hours
Rib Eye, 4 to 6 lbs. (Roast at 350°)	140°	1½ to 1¾ hours
	160°	1¾ hours
	170°	2 hours
Tenderloin whole 4 to 6 lbs. (Roast at 425°)	140°	¾ to 1 hour

BAKE-ALONG IDEA:	Baked Rutabaga Puff *
DIVIDEND IDEAS:	Beef Curry *
	Stuffed Beef Rolls *
	Beef Hash Au Gratin *

*Recipes given

BAKED RUTABAGA PUFF

3 c. mashed cooked rutabagas
1 tsp. salt
⅛ tsp. pepper
2 tsp. sugar
¼ c. melted butter
2 eggs, slightly beaten
1 c. fresh bread crumbs

Combine rutabagas, salt, pepper, sugar, butter and eggs in bowl. Whip until well blended. Stir in bread crumbs. Turn onto greased 1-qt. casserole.

Bake in 325° oven 50 minutes or until lightly browned and puffy. Makes 6 servings.

BEEF CURRY

½ c. chopped green onions
1 c. chopped celery
½ c. butter
½ c. flour
2 c. light cream
3 beef bouillon cubes
2 c. boiling water
1 small green pepper, cut in strips
2 tsp. curry powder
⅛ tsp. ground ginger
⅛ tsp. pepper
4 c. cubed cooked beef
Fluffy cooked rice

Cook green onions and celery in melted butter in heavy saucepan until onion is tender. Blend in flour. Stir in light cream. Dissolve bouillon cubes in boiling water. Add to flour mixture. Cook over medium heat, stirring constantly, until sauce is bubbling and thickened. Stir in green pepper, curry powder, ginger, pepper and beef. Continue cooking, stirring constantly, until mixture is thoroughly heated. Serve on fluffy rice. Makes 6 to 8 servings.

STUFFED BEEF ROLLS

½ c. chopped onion
½ (8 oz.) pkg. herb-seasoned stuffing
   mix
6 large thin slices roast beef
½ c. dairy sour cream
1 (10½ oz.) can condensed cream of
   mushroom soup
Grated Parmesan cheese

Add onion to stuffing mix. Prepare stuffing according to package directions. Spoon onto beef slices and bring sides of each up over stuffing, overlapping edges in center. Place, seam side down, in a row in greased 11x7x1½-inch baking dish. Blend sour cream into soup and spoon over rolls.

Bake in 350° oven 20 to 25 minutes or until thoroughly heated. Sprinkle Parmesan cheese over rolls. Bake 5 more minutes. Makes 6 servings.

BEEF HASH AU GRATIN

¼ c. finely chopped onion
¼ c. chopped green pepper
¼ c. butter
1 tblsp. flour
⅛ tsp. pepper
1 tsp. dry mustard
1 tsp. instant beef bouillon powder
1 c. water
1 tsp. Worcestershire sauce
3 c. finely chopped cooked beef
3 c. finely chopped cooked potatoes
1 c. shredded Cheddar cheese

Cook onion and green pepper in melted butter in large skillet until onion is tender. Blend in flour, pepper, mustard and bouillon powder. Stir in water and Worcestershire sauce. Cook over medium heat, stirring constantly, until sauce is thick and bubbling. Stir in beef and potatoes. Divide mixture among 6 greased individual ramekins or spoon into greased large shallow casserole.

Bake in 350° oven, 15 minutes for ramekins, 20 minutes for large casserole. Top with shredded cheese. Makes 6 servings.

ROAST PORK

Select preferred cut of pork for roasting. Do not cover. Roast in 325° for following approximate times or to desired internal degree of doneness.

Cut and Weight	Internal Temp. on Removal from Oven	Approximate Cooking Time
Loin, center, 3 to 5 lbs.	170°	2½ to 3 hours
Loin, half, 5 to 7 lbs.	170°	3½ to 4¼ hours
Loin, blade end, 3 to 4 lbs.	170°	2¼ to 2¾ hours
Loin, center, boneless, rolled 3 to 4 lbs.	170°	2½ to 3 hours
Shoulder, bone-in, 4 to 6 lbs.	185°	3 to 3½ hours
Shoulder, boneless, rolled, 3 to 5 lbs.	185°	3 to 3½ hours
Leg (fresh ham), 10 to 14 lbs.	185°	5½ to 6½ hours
Leg, half (fresh ham), 5 to 7 lbs.	185°	4 to 4½ hours

BAKE-ALONG IDEA: Cabbage Carrot Bake *
DIVIDEND IDEAS: Belgian Pork Skillet *
                   Sweet-Sour Pork *
                   Quick Chop Suey *

* Recipes given

CABBAGE CARROT BAKE

3 medium carrots, pared
6 c. shredded cabbage
Salt
Pepper
2 tblsp. minced onion
½ c. water

Cut carrots into thin strips using vegetable parer. Arrange cabbage and carrot strips in 2-qt. casserole. Season with salt and pepper. Sprinkle with onion. Add water. Cover.

Bake in 325° oven 35 to 40 minutes or until vegetables are tender. Makes 6 to 8 servings.

BELGIAN PORK SKILLET

2 (10 oz.) pkgs. frozen Brussels sprouts
    or 1¾ lbs. fresh
6 slices roast pork, ½ inch thick
2 tblsp. butter
1 tblsp. flour
1 tsp. instant chicken bouillon powder
1 tsp. dill weed
¾ c. water

Cook Brussels sprouts in lightly salted water until just tender. Drain.

Quickly brown pork slices on both sides in melted butter in heavy skillet. Remove and keep warm. Reserve drippings. Blend flour, chicken bouillon powder and dill weed into reserved drippings. Stir in water. Cook over medium heat, stirring constantly, until mixture bubbles and is thickened. Gently stir in Brussels sprouts. Top with pork slices. Cover and cook over low heat for about 5 minutes or until thoroughly heated. Makes 6 servings.

SWEET-SOUR PORK

⅓ c. sugar
1 tsp. salt
⅓ c. vinegar
2 c. water
3 tblsp. cornstarch
½ c. water
3 c. cubed cooked pork
2 tsp. soy sauce
2 small carrots, thinly sliced
1 small green pepper, cut in thin strips
2 small tomatoes, cut in eighths
1 (8½ oz.) can pineapple chunks, drained
Fluffy cooked rice or chow mein noodles

Combine sugar, salt, vinegar and 2 c. water in large saucepan. Bring to boiling. Blend cornstarch and remaining ½ c. water; mix well. Stir into first mixture. Cook over low heat, stirring constantly, until sauce bubbles and is thickened. Add pork; simmer 7 minutes.

Stir in soy sauce. Gently stir in carrots, green pepper, tomatoes and pineapple. Cook for about 5 more minutes to heat thoroughly. Serve over rice or chow mein noodles. Makes 5 to 6 servings.

QUICK CHOP SUEY

2 c. cooked pork strips
½ c. chopped onion
2 tblsp. butter
1 c. bias-cut celery
½ medium green pepper, cut in thin strips
½ tsp. salt
⅛ tsp. pepper
2 c. chicken broth
1 (1 lb.) can bean sprouts, drained
3 tblsp. cornstarch
3 tblsp. cold water
2 tsp. Worcestershire sauce
1 tblsp. soy sauce
1 tblsp. molasses
4 c. cooked rice

Cook pork and onion in butter in skillet about 5 minutes or until meat is browned and onion is tender. Stir in celery, green pepper, salt, pepper, chicken broth and bean sprouts. Cover and cook over low heat about 5 minutes or until heated through.

Combine cornstarch and water in small jar. Add Worcestershire sauce, soy sauce and molasses. Cover and shake jar well. Stir into meat mixture. Cook, stirring lightly, 3 to 4 minutes or until mixture is clear and thickened. Serve in ring of rice. Makes 6 servings.

CHAPTER V

Head Start on Entertaining

If you plan your party menu carefully, your oven can function almost as well as extra help in the kitchen. Feature a make-ahead dish that can be refrigerated or frozen. Do a bread and a dessert at the same time. With this type of menu, entertaining is easy on the hostess. You simply let the oven take over while you enjoy visiting with your guests.

Refrigerated dishes will take slightly longer to heat than if prepared and baked non-stop. Time will depend on contents of dish and how long it requires heat to penetrate the cold food.

Frozen dishes will take almost half again as long to heat. You can shorten the heating time for a frozen make-ahead main dish, by transferring it from the freezer to the refrigerator a day in advance of the party so that it can partially thaw before baking.

Chill cold beverages ahead of time and, if you're serving iced drinks, put filled ice bucket, tongs and glasses on a large tray in a handy spot for self service.

Pre-load the coffeemaker so you can plug it in just before you remove the food from the oven.

The key to carefree entertaining, especially for a crowd, is to keep the menu simple and a menu that is easy to serve. If guests are not seated at a table, make the food easy to eat as well. In this case, avoid foods that need to be cut with a knife; pre-butter the bread or rolls. Avoid molded salads as they tend to melt and run together with hot foods on the plates.

MENU 1

FIRESIDE FARE

Party Chili *
Assorted Crackers
Celery Curls   Ripe Olives   Carrot Sticks
"Top Banana" Cake *
Ice Cream
Coffee   Milk

*Recipes given

With this flavorful, meaty chili ready and waiting in the freezer, the most impromptu party can be a snap. If time allows, partially or completely thaw the chili in the refrigerator first. This will cut reheating time, of course. It's a substantial, thick chili, so you may want to add a little tomato juice before you put it in the oven to heat, to prevent sticking. Take the "Top Banana" Cake (see Index for recipe) from the freezer, too, for an easily achieved happy ending to the party.

PARTY CHILI

---

2 lbs. lean ground beef
2 tsp. salt
2 c. chopped onion
2 cloves garlic, minced
1 (1 lb. 12 oz.) can tomatoes
2 (8 oz.) cans tomato sauce
2 (1 lb.) cans kidney beans, drained
2 to 3 tsp. chili powder
¼ tsp. paprika
1 tsp. basil leaves
1 tsp. sugar

Brown ground beef in Dutch oven. Add salt, onion, and garlic; cook until onion is tender. Stir in tomatoes, tomato sauce, kidney beans, chili powder, paprika, basil and sugar. Cover. Simmer 2 to 2½ hours. If you like a thinner chili, add tomato juice or water. Makes about 8 (1½-c.) servings.

To freeze: Cool quickly and place in freezer containers. Cover tightly. Seal, label and freeze.

To reheat: Thaw in refrigerator. Turn into 3-qt. casserole. Cover. Heat in 400° oven about 40 minutes.

MENU 2

SUPPER, ITALIAN-STYLE

Lasagne Rolls *
Tossed Green Salad
Oil and Vinegar Dressing
Hot Italian Bread
Italian Cream Cake *
Red Wine
Coffee

* Recipes given

This is the popular Italian lasagne, but the noodles are rolled instead of layered, and the results are tastier then ever! A make-ahead to refrigerate or freeze and then turn over to the oven for carefree heating at party-time. Heat foil-wrapped bread, pre-sliced and buttered alongside. With a big green salad all ready for last-minute tossing, and with Italian Cream Cake (see Index for recipe) from the refrigerator, your meal is a breeze to prepare.

LASAGNE ROLLS

1 lb. lean ground beef
½ lb. Italian pork sausage
2 tblsp. cooking oil
2 small cloves garlic, minced
1 tsp. basil leaves
1 tsp. salt
⅛ tsp. pepper
1 (4 oz.) can mushroom stems and pieces
1 (1 lb.) can tomatoes
2 (6 oz.) cans tomato paste
10 oz. lasagne noodles
2 eggs, slightly beaten
1 lb. cream-style cottage cheese
1 (3 oz.) pkg. cream cheese, softened
½ c. grated Parmesan cheese
1 tblsp. dried parsley flakes
1 tsp. salt
⅛ tsp. pepper
1 c. shredded mozzarella cheese

Brown beef and sausage in hot cooking oil in large heavy skillet. Pour off excess fat. Stir in garlic, basil, 1 tsp. salt, ⅛ tsp. pepper, mushrooms, tomatoes and tomato paste. Simmer, uncovered, 30 minutes; stir occasionally.

Cook noodles according to package directions. Drain and rinse with cold water. Combine eggs, cottage cheese, cream cheese, Parmesan cheese, parsley, 1 tsp. salt and ⅛ tsp. pepper in bowl; mix well. Spread each noodle with some of the egg-cheese mixture. Roll up jelly-roll fashion. Place, seam side down, in rows in 13x9x2-inch baking pan. Pour meat sauce over rolls and sprinkle with mozzarella cheese.

Bake in 350° oven 25 to 30 minutes. Makes about 12 servings.

To freeze: Cool meat sauce quickly. Pour over lasagne rolls in baking pan. Cover tightly with aluminum foil. Seal, label and freeze.

To reheat: Thaw in refrigerator. Heat, covered, in 375° oven 35 to 40 minutes. Sprinkle on mozzarella cheese and return to oven, uncovered, for 5 more minutes.

MENU 3

COMPANY BRUNCH

Citrus Coolers
Shrimp Crepes with Mushroom Sauce *
Asparagus Vinaigrette
on Romaine
Assorted Sweet Rolls *
Coffee

* Recipes given

Here's an ideal menu for Sunday or holiday brunch or luncheon. Make the Shrimp Crepes ahead and refrigerate or freeze. Then pop in the oven to heat while guests are enjoying their Citrus Coolers. (Blend together 3 parts orange juice, 2 parts tomato juice and 1 part lemon juice, and serve over ice.) Heat the sweet rolls from the freezer, too, to bring piping hot to the table. Plug in the coffeemaker and arrange salads just before crepes are finished baking.

SHRIMP CREPES WITH MUSHROOM SAUCE

1 egg
¾ c. milk
1 tblsp. melted butter
¾ c. unsifted flour
¼ c. finely chopped celery
1 tsp. instant minced onion
2 c. finely chopped cooked shrimp
¼ c. butter
¼ c. flour
1 c. chicken broth
1 c. light cream
¾ tsp. salt
¼ tsp. pepper
2 tblsp. dried parsley flakes
1 (4 oz.) can mushroom stems and pieces
Parmesan cheese

Beat egg well in small bowl. Stir in milk, 1 tblsp. butter and ¾ c. flour. Beat with rotary beater until smooth. Pour 2 tblsp. of batter into well-greased 7-inch skillet, tilting pan so batter will spread evenly. Bake 1 minute, until edges of crepe begin to curl. Turn, bake on other side about 1 minute. Slide crepe onto plate.

Repeat with remaining batter, greasing pan each time before adding batter. If batter begins to thicken, stir in a little milk. Makes 8 (7-inch) crepes.

Combine celery, onion and shrimp in mixing bowl. Melt ¼ c. butter in skillet; blend in ¼ c. flour. Stir in broth and light cream. Cook, stirring constantly, until sauce is bubbling and thickened. Stir in salt, pepper and parsley flakes.

Combine ¾ c. of the sauce with the shrimp mixture.

Add undrained mushrooms to remaining sauce. Spread about ¼ c. shrimp mixture down center of each crepe. Roll up. Place seam side down in greased 11x7x1½-inch baking dish. Pour remaining mushroom sauce over crepes and sprinkle with Parmesan cheese.

Bake in 375° oven 20 minutes. Makes 4 servings.

To freeze: Cool sauce quickly and proceed as above, placing filled crepes in freezer-to-oven ware baking dish or baking pan. Pour sauce over crepes. Cover tightly with aluminum foil. Seal, label and freeze.

To reheat: Thaw in refrigerator. Heat in 375° oven about 25 minutes, sprinkle with Parmesan cheese and return to oven for 5 more minutes.

MENU 4

"PACKET" SUPPER

Packet Chicken *
Creamy Coleslaw
Tomato Slices
Toasted Cornbread Squares
Peanut Butter Ice Cream Pie *
Coffee   Milk

* Recipes given

You can refrigerate or freeze individual heavy-duty aluminum foil pouches of browned chicken with a flavorful sweet-sour sauce, then bake them while the party's in progress. After you remove the chicken, "up" the oven and toast split squares of cornbread, made in advance. Transfer the Peanut Butter Ice Cream Pie (see Index for recipe) from the freezer to the refrigerator to temper about 15 minutes before serving.

PACKET CHICKEN

> 2 (2½ to 3 lb.) broiler-fryers, cut up
> ½ c. cooking oil
> ½ c. chopped onion
> ½ c. brown sugar, firmly packed
> 2 tsp. dry mustard
> 2 tsp. salt
> ⅛ tsp. pepper
> ½ c. lemon juice

Lightly brown chicken in hot oil in heavy skillet. (Save necks, backs and giblets for use in making soup.) While chicken is browning, tear off 8 pieces of heavy-duty aluminum foil, about 18x14 inches each.

Place chicken piece or pieces in center of each sheet of foil, dividing chicken equally. Add onion to skillet, cook until onion is tender. Stir in brown sugar, mustard, salt, pepper and lemon juice. Spoon mixture over chicken pieces. Bring 4 corners of each sheet of foil up over chicken, joining at top. Press foil close to chicken. To seal, fold over ends of foil and press to package. Place packets in shallow baking pan.

Bake in 375° oven 45 to 50 minutes or until chicken is tender. Makes 8 servings.

To freeze: Place pan of chicken packets in freezer. When chicken is solidly frozen, remove pan.

To reheat: Place frozen packets in baking pan. Bake in 375° oven 1 hour and 10 minutes or until chicken is tender.

MENU 5

SNACK-TIME SPECIAL

Cheddar Cheese Soup
Hot Ham Snack Loaf *
Fresh Fruit Bowl   Cookies
Coffee   Milk

* Recipes given

French bread, sliced and spread with a zippy ham filling, then foil-wrapped and frozen, can be a most sat-
isfactory solution to the call for hurry-up snacks. While
it's in the oven, heat canned Cheddar cheese soup and
serve in large mugs or soup bowls.

HOT HAM SNACK LOAF

---

    3 c. ground cooked ham
    ¼ c. finely minced onion
    ½ c. mayonnaise
    ¼ c. prepared mustard
    1 loaf French or Vienna bread, about
        18 inches long
    ½ c. butter, softened

Blend together ham, onion, mayonnaise and mustard
in bowl. Cut loaf in diagonal ¾-inch slices, cutting to
within about ½-inch of bottom crust. Spread one side of
each slice with butter and then the ham mixture. Wrap
loaf in aluminum foil.

Bake in 350° oven about 20 minutes or until thoroughly heated. Serve hot. Makes 8 servings.

To freeze: Place foil-wrapped loaf in freezer.

To reheat: Heat frozen foil-wrapped loaf in 375° oven 30 to 35 minutes.

MENU 6

PARTY LUNCHEON

Hot Deviled Turkey Sandwiches *
Tossed Green Salad
Baked Alaska Cranberry Pie *
Coffee   Milk

* Recipes given

Elegant and hearty ham and turkey sandwiches to prepare shortly in advance of serving. Refrigerate until party time and then quickly heat. A rich Cheddar cheese sauce adds extra flavor. Do the Alaska Cranberry Pie in advance, too. It will hold nicely in the freezer for two days before browning in a 475° oven just before serving (see Index for recipe).

HOT DEVILED TURKEY SANDWICHES

---

4 English muffins, split
1 (3¼ oz.) can deviled ham
16 medium slices cooked turkey
2 tblsp. butter
2 tblsp. flour
½ tsp. salt
¼ tsp. dry mustard
1 tsp. Worcestershire sauce
1 c. milk
1 c. shredded Cheddar cheese
¼ c. grated Romano cheese

Lightly toast English muffins. Spread each with deviled ham. Place in individual shallow casseroles or in shallow baking pan. Top each half with two slices of turkey. Cover with plastic wrap and refrigerate.

Melt butter in saucepan. Blend in flour, salt, mustard and Worcestershire sauce. Add milk. Cook over medium heat, stirring constantly, until sauce bubbles and is thickened. Add Cheddar cheese; stir until melted. Remove from heat. Pour into bowl or plastic container. Cover and refrigerate.

To heat sandwiches, spoon sauce over turkey and sprinkle with Romano cheese.

Bake in 350° oven 20 to 25 minutes or until thoroughly heated. Makes 8 servings.

MENU 7

AFTER THE GAME SPECIAL

Macaroni Cheese Bake *
Sliced Cucumber Salad
Rolls   Butter
Chocolate Ice Cream Roll *
Coffee   Milk

* Recipes given

Refrigerate this creamy casserole ahead and serve to armchair sport fans either during or after the big game. So easy on the hostess, too. Simply reheat the casserole and warm the rolls. Serve the yummy Chocolate Ice Cream Roll right from the freezer (see Index for recipe).

MACARONI CHEESE BAKE

2 c. chopped onion
½ c. butter
2 tsp. Worcestershire sauce
1 tsp. salt
¼ tsp. pepper
¼ tsp. dry mustard
4 tblsp. flour
2 c. milk
1 lb. Cheddar cheese, shredded
2 (1 lb.) cans stewed tomatoes, drained
8 oz. elbow macaroni, cooked and drained

Saute onion in melted butter in 3-qt. saucepan until tender (do not brown). Add Worcestershire sauce, salt, pepper, mustard and flour. Cook, stirring constantly, until mixture is smooth and bubbly. Remove from heat. Gradually stir in milk. Cook over medium heat, stirring constantly, until mixture comes to a boil. Boil 1 minute. Add cheese; stir until melted. Stir in tomatoes. Place alternate layers of macaroni and sauce in greased 3-qt. casserole.

Bake in 375° oven 35 minutes or until bubbly. Makes 6 servings.

To refrigerate: Cover casserole with aluminum foil and refrigerate.

To reheat: Uncover. Bake in 375° oven 50 minutes or until bubbly.

CHAPTER VI

Make-Ahead Dishes That Carry Well

The foods that are served at picnics, community and church suppers and family reunions are often the focal point of the event. That's when you want to fix the dish that will rate "superior" with the guests.

You will never go wrong if you bake a hearty main dish. Perhaps a big pan of light, tender meatballs in a rich gravy or an out-of-the-ordinary meat loaf. Casseroles and hearty stews are always welcome.

Social activities often arrive in bunches—just when your schedule is especially crowded and hectic. Why not plan a leisurely day of baking and freezing several of your renowned specialties and then you'll be ahead of the push.

Freezer-to-oven ware allows you to freeze and bake in the same casserole non-stop—a distinct advantage, even though reheating time is rather long. If you'd like to cut down on the time, you might want to at least partially thaw the casserole in the refrigerator first.

The regular type of casserole ware will not withstand sharp contrasts in temperature. So freeze the mixture in rigid plastic containers, then transfer to a casserole when you're ready to use it.

Leave the food in the plastic container to thaw—partially or completely—in the refrigerator, then transfer the thawed mixture to the casserole. If you like, add shredded cheese, buttered crumbs or other topping before baking.

ITALIAN MEATBALLS

2 c. chopped onion
4 cloves garlic, minced
¼ c. cooking oil
¼ c. chopped fresh parsley
2 tsp. basil leaves
4 (1 lb. 12 oz.) cans tomatoes, cut up
4 (6 oz.) cans tomato paste
1 tblsp. salt
½ tsp. pepper
1 tsp. sugar
2 c. water
10 slices bread
1 c. water
2 lbs. lean ground beef
1 lb. lean ground pork
4 eggs, slightly beaten
¼ c. chopped fresh parsley
3 small cloves garlic, minced
1 tblsp. salt
¼ tsp. pepper
¼ c. cooking oil
Cooked spaghetti, noodles or rice

Cook onion and 4 cloves garlic in ¼ c. hot oil in large Dutch oven until onion is tender. Stir in ¼ c. parsley, basil, tomatoes, tomato paste, 1 tblsp. salt, ½ tsp. pepper, sugar and 2 c. water. Bring to a boil. Simmer, uncovered, 1½ to 2 hours, stirring occasionally.

While sauce is cooking, prepare meatballs. Soak bread slices in 1 c. water in shallow pan. Squeeze out excess liquid. Combine bread, beef, pork, eggs, ¼ c. parsley, 3 cloves garlic, 1 tblsp. salt and ¼ tsp. pepper in bowl. Mix lightly, but well. Place meat mixture on sheet of waxed paper, cover with second sheet and flatten meat mixture to rectangle. Cut in 72 squares. Wet fingers and shape each square into ball. Brown meatballs in ¼ c. hot cooking oil in heavy skillet. Remove meatballs as they brown.

Add meatballs to sauce and simmer, covered, 1 more hour.* Serve over cooked spaghetti, noodles or rice. Makes 16 to 18 servings.

*To freeze: Cool quickly and place in freezer containers. Cover tightly. Seal, label and freeze.

To reheat: Thaw in refrigerator. Turn into two 2-qt. casseroles or two 11x7x1½-inch baking dishes. Cover and heat in 400° oven about 40 minutes or until heated. Serve over cooked spaghetti, noodles or rice.

Bake-along Ideas: Potatoes
                        Muffins
                        Fruit Cobbler

INDIVIDUAL HAM LOAVES

    1½ lbs. ground fresh pork
    1 lb. ground smoked ham
    2 c. saltine crumbs
    1 c. milk
    2 eggs, slightly beaten
    2 tsp. dry mustard
    ¾ c. brown sugar, firmly packed
    ½ c. vinegar
    ½ c. water

Combine pork, ham, saltine crumbs, milk and eggs. Shape into 10 loaves and place in shallow baking pan. Blend together mustard, brown sugar, vinegar and water in bowl. Pour over ham loaves.*

Bake in 350° oven 45 to 50 minutes, basting loaves with sauce twice during baking. Makes 10 servings.
*To freeze: Cover baking pan with aluminum foil. Seal, label and freeze.
To bake: Do not thaw. Bake, uncovered, in 375° oven 1 to 1¼ hours. Baste loaves with sauce once or twice during baking.

Bake-along Ideas: Macaroni and Cheese
Baked Apples or Pears
Gingerbread

TURKEY TETRAZZINI

½ c. butter
¼ c. chopped green pepper
¾ c. flour
6 c. chicken broth
2 c. light cream
2 tblsp. lemon juice
2 tsp. salt
¼ tsp. pepper
6 c. cubed cooked turkey
1 (8 oz.) can sliced mushrooms, drained
1 lb. spaghetti, cooked and drained
Grated Parmesan cheese

Melt butter in heavy Dutch oven. Add green pepper; cook 3 to 4 minutes or until tender. Blend in flour. Gradually stir in chicken broth and cream. Cook over medium heat, stirring constantly, until sauce bubbles and is thickened. Blend in lemon juice, salt and pepper. Remove from heat. Gently combine sauce with turkey, mushrooms and spaghetti.* Turn into two 13x9x2-inch baking dishes and sprinkle with Parmesan cheese.

Bake in 375° oven 20 to 25 minutes or until hot. Makes 10 to 12 servings.

*To freeze: Cool mixture quickly. Place in freezer containers and cover tightly. Seal, label and freeze.

To reheat: Thaw mixture in refrigerator. Bake, uncovered, in 375° oven 35 to 45 minutes or until hot.

Bake-along Ideas: Quick Coffee Cake
                                  Fruit Crisp or Betty
                                  Vegetable Casserole

EASY OVEN STEW

4 lbs. boneless beef chuck, cut in
   1-inch cubes
¼ tsp. garlic salt
2 tsp. salt
¼ tsp. pepper
1 tsp. marjoram leaves
4 medium onions, sliced
6 medium carrots, pared and sliced
2 tsp. instant beef bouillon powder
1½ c. hot water
¼ c. lemon juice
2 (8 oz.) cans tomato sauce
1 (14 oz.) pkg. corn muffin mix

Place beef in greased large baking pan. Combine garlic salt, salt, pepper and marjoram; sprinkle over beef. Arrange onions and carrots on top. Mix together bouillon powder, water, lemon juice and tomato sauce in bowl; pour over meat and vegetables. Cover.

Bake in 350° oven about 1¾ hours or until meat is tender.*

Remove from oven. Increase heat to 400°. Prepare corn muffin mix according to package directions and drop by tablespoonfuls on top of meat. Return to oven and bake, uncovered, 15 more minutes. Makes about 12 servings.

*To freeze: Cool stew quickly. Place in freezer containers and cover tightly. Seal, label and freeze.

To reheat: Thaw in refrigerator. Transfer to two 11x7x1½-inch baking dishes. Cover and heat in 400° oven about 30 minutes. Remove from oven. Top with corn muffin batter as in main recipe. Return to oven. Bake in 400° oven 15 more minutes.

Bake-along Ideas: Bar Cookies
Applesauce Loaf Cake
Bread Pudding

CHICKEN-HAM-RICE CASSEROLE

½ c. finely chopped onion
1 c. chopped celery
¼ c. butter
6 tblsp. flour
1 tsp. salt
⅛ tsp. pepper
½ tsp. poultry seasoning
1 tsp. Worcestershire sauce
2½ c. chicken broth
4 c. cubed cooked chicken
2 c. cubed cooked ham
2 c. cooked rice
1 c. shredded Cheddar cheese

Cook onion and celery in melted butter in large skillet 4 to 5 minutes or until onion is tender. Blend in flour, salt, pepper, poultry seasoning and Worcester-shire sauce. Gradually stir in chicken broth. Cook over medium heat, stirring constantly, until sauce bubbles and is thickened. Gently stir in chicken, ham and rice.* Turn into greased 3-qt. casserole.

Bake in 350° oven 30 minutes. Sprinkle with cheese and bake 10 more minutes. Makes 10 to 12 servings.

*To freeze: Cool mixture quickly, place in freezer containers and cover tightly. Seal, label and freeze.

To reheat: Thaw in refrigerator. Turn into 3-qt casserole and bake in 350° oven 45 to 50 minutes. Sprinkle with cheese and bake 10 more minutes.

Bake-along Ideas: Winter Squash
                                Prune Whip
                                Upside-down Cake

BAKED LIMAS WITH SMOKED SAUSAGE

---

      2 lbs. dried baby lima beans
      3 qts. water
      2 large onions, coarsely chopped
      ½ lb. bacon, cut up
      ½ c. molasses
      2 tsp. Worcestershire sauce
      1 tblsp. salt
      ¼ tsp. pepper
      ½ tsp. ground cloves
      1 tblsp. dry mustard
      ¼ c. vinegar
      3 lbs. smoked sausage links

Wash beans. Soak beans overnight in water in Dutch oven. Stir in onion, bacon, molasses and Worcestershire sauce. Blend in salt, pepper, cloves and mustard. Bring mixture to boiling. Reduce heat, cover and simmer 30 minutes. Stir in vinegar. Turn into two 13x9x2-inch baking pans.

Bake, uncovered, in 325° oven 2 hours or until beans are tender. Stir once or twice during baking and add a little more water, if necessary.*

Arrange sausage links on top of beans and return to oven for 15 more minutes. Makes about 12 servings.

*To freeze: Cool beans quickly, place in freezer containers and cover tightly. Seal, label and freeze.

To reheat: Thaw in refrigerator. Turn mixture into two 13x9x2-inch baking pans. Cover. Bake in 375° oven 30 minutes. Remove from oven, top with sausage links. Bake, uncovered, 15 more minutes.

Bake-along Ideas: Baked Custard
Steamed Dried Fruit
Rice Pudding

CHAPTER VII

Bake-Ahead
Breads and Cookies

Nothing smells better than the delicious aroma of homemade cookies and breads baking in the oven. And everyone prefers homemade baked goodies to the store-bought variety. An easy way to keep the cookie jar filled and a few extra treats in the freezer is to enlist the help of the family in a baking marathon. The youngsters will enjoy a Bake-In Day and will be proud of the results.

After deciding beforehand the recipes you'll use and the order in which to prepare them so as to best utilize the oven, make a simple chart listing the amounts of ingredients needed for the various recipes. Many of the ingredients—flour, sugar, salt, leavening, butter or shortening, eggs—will be common to them all, so set up a "central supply" in one counter area.

Put measuring equipment, sifter and all necessary utensils on a large tray, and line up pans, cookie sheets, spatulas and cooling racks. Set out butter and eggs ahead of time to come to room temperature.

To reduce the mess and clutter, reserve counter space for kneading, rolling and cutting, and another area for cooling and packaging the product.

Let one youngster measure all the dry ingredients for each recipe, and place them on sheets of waxed paper labeled with the recipe name. Another one can grate chocolate, chop nuts and grease pans. With an assembly line plan, you can accomplish twice as much and the family will share in the fun.

Systematize the packaging. Use rigid plastic or metal containers with tight-fitting covers, moisture-vapor proof wraps, and have labeling materials handy. If you are freezing cookie dough, wrap or pack it to exclude all moisture and air, so quality will hold during storage. Don't freeze highly-spiced doughs, as they undergo flavor changes during storage.

As you put the breads and cookies in the freezer, date them and enter each package and date in an inventory book. It's a handy reminder to serve the foods at peak quality.

OLD-FASHIONED RAISIN BREAD

1½ c. buttermilk
1 pkg. active dry yeast
¼ c. sugar
2 eggs, slightly beaten
½ c. shortening, melted and cooled
5 to 5½ c. unsifted flour
1½ tsp. salt
½ tsp. baking soda
1 c. raisins

Heat buttermilk in saucepan to warm (115°F.). Pour into mixing bowl. Add yeast and sugar; stir until yeast is dissolved. Add eggs and shortening to buttermilk mixture; mix well.

Sift together flour, salt and baking soda. Add by thirds to buttermilk mixture, beating well after each addition. Turn dough onto well-floured surface. Knead until dough is smooth and elastic. Knead in raisins.

Place dough in greased bowl, turning dough once to grease surface. Cover and let rise in warm place until doubled, about 1 hour.

Punch down dough and turn out onto floured surface. Divide dough in half; let rest 10 to 15 minutes. Shape into loaves; place in two greased 8½x4½x2½-inch pans. Cover and let rise until doubled, about 1 hour.

Bake in 375° oven 40 to 50 minutes or until done. If bread browns too quickly, cover loosely with aluminum foil. Remove from pans; cool on racks. Makes 2 loaves.

SWEDISH LIMPA

2 pkgs. active dry yeast
½ c. warm water (115°F.)
1 c. warm water (115°F.)
¼ c. molasses
⅓ c. sugar
1 tblsp. salt
2 tblsp. grated orange rind
2 tblsp. soft shortening
2 c. medium rye flour
3½ c. unsifted flour

Sprinkle yeast over ½ c. warm water; stir to dissolve. Combine 1 c. warm water, molasses, sugar, salt and orange rind. Stir in shortening, yeast mixture and rye flour. Gradually beat in enough white flour to make a stiff dough. Turn out onto floured surface. Knead until smooth and elastic, about 8 to 10 minutes. Place dough in greased bowl, turning dough once to grease surface. Cover and let rise in warm place until doubled.

Punch down dough and shape into two round loaves. Place at opposite corners of lightly greased baking sheet. Let rise in warm place until doubled.

Bake in 375° oven 35 minutes or until done. Remove from baking sheet; cool on racks. Makes 2 loaves.

CHEDDAR CHEESE BREAD

1 pkg. active dry yeast
¼ c. warm water (115°F.)
2 c. milk
2 tblsp. sugar
2 tsp. salt
2 tblsp. shortening
5½ to 6 c. unsifted flour
2 c. shredded Cheddar cheese

Soften yeast in warm water. Combine milk, sugar, salt and shortening in saucepan and heat to warm (115°F.). Pour into mixing bowl. Stir in about 2 c. of flour; beat well. Blend in yeast mixture; beat well. Mix in enough remaining flour to make moderately stiff dough. Mix in cheese.

Turn out onto lightly floured surface and knead until smooth and satiny, about 8 to 10 minutes. Place in lightly greased bowl, turning dough once to grease surface. Cover and let rise in warm place until doubled, about 1 hour.

Punch down dough. Divide into 2 portions. Shape in loaves and place in two greased 9x5x3-inch loaf pans. Cover and let rise in warm place until doubled, about 45 to 60 minutes.

Bake in 375° oven 35 to 40 minutes or until done. (If top crust browns too quickly, cover loosely with foil after 20 minutes of baking time.) Makes 2 loaves.

OATMEAL BREAD

1½ c. boiling water
1 c. quick-cooking oats
½ c. dark molasses
2 tsp. salt
3 tblsp. shortening
2 pkgs. active dry yeast
½ c. warm water (115°F.)
5½ to 6 c. unsifted flour
1 tblsp. water
1 egg white, slightly beaten
Quick-cooking oats

Pour boiling water over 1 c. oats in large mixing bowl. Stir in molasses, salt and shortening and cool to warm (115°F.). Soften yeast in warm water. Stir 2 c. flour into oatmeal mixture; beat well. Add softened yeast; beat well. Mix in enough flour to make a moderately stiff dough.

Turn out onto floured surface and knead until smooth, about 10 to 12 minutes. (Dough will be slightly sticky.) Place in greased bowl, turning dough once to grease surface. Cover and let rise in warm place until doubled, about 1 hour.

Punch down dough. Divide in half and shape in loaves. Place in two greased 9x5x3-inch loaf pans. Cover and let rise in warm place until doubled, 45 to 60 minutes. Beat water into egg white and brush on tops of loaves. Sprinkle lightly with additional rolled oats.

Bake in 375° oven 35 to 40 minutes or until done. (If top crust browns too quickly, cover loaves loosely with foil after 20 minutes of baking time.) Makes 2 loaves.

PUMPERNICKEL

½ c. yellow cornmeal
¾ c. cold water
1 c. boiling water
1 c. hot mashed potatoes
1 tblsp. sugar
1 tblsp. salt
2 tblsp. soft shortening
1 tblsp. caraway seeds
2 pkgs. active dry yeast
½ c. warm water (115°F.)
3½ c. pumpernickel rye flour
2 to 2½ c. unsifted flour

Stir cornmeal into cold water in saucepan. Add boiling water. Cook over medium heat, stirring constantly, until mixture is smooth and thick. Remove from heat. Stir in mashed potatoes, sugar, salt, shortening and caraway seeds; mix well.

Soften yeast in warm water. Blend into cornmeal mixture. Gradually stir in rye flour. Beat in enough flour to make a stiff dough.

Turn out on floured surface and knead until smooth, 10 to 12 minutes. Place in greased bowl, turning dough once to grease surface. Cover and let rise in warm place until doubled, 1 to 1½ hours.

Punch down dough. Divide in half and shape in two round loaves. Place on lightly greased baking sheet sprinkled with cornmeal. Cover and let rise until doubled, 45 minutes to 1 hour.

Bake in 375° oven 10 minutes. Reduce heat to 350° and bake 30 to 35 more minutes. Makes 2 loaves.

BASIC SWEET DOUGH

> **2 pkgs. active dry yeast**
> **¼ c. warm water (115°F.)**
> **1 c. milk, scalded**
> **½ c. sugar**
> **2 tsp. salt**
> **¼ c. shortening**
> **5 to 5½ c. unsifted flour**
> **2 eggs, well beaten**

Sprinkle yeast over warm water; stir to dissolve. Combine milk, sugar, salt and shortening in mixing bowl. Cool to lukewarm. Add 2 c. flour and mix well. Add yeast mixture and eggs; beat well. Mix in enough remaining flour to make a soft dough. Turn out onto well-floured surface. Knead until smooth and satiny, about 8 to 10 minutes. Place dough in lightly greased bowl, turning once to grease surface. Cover and let rise in warm place until doubled, about 1½ hours.

Punch down dough. Divide in half. Shape into any of the variations that follow. Cover and let rise until doubled, about 1 hour. Bake as directed.

ORANGE LOAF: Use ½ of Basic Sweet Dough. Pat or roll into rectangle 8-inches wide and ¼-inch thick. Brush with melted butter. Sprinkle with 1 tblsp. grated orange rind and ¼ c. sugar. Roll as for jelly roll from 8-inch side. Place in greased 8½x4½x2½-inch loaf pan. Cover and let rise until doubled, about 45 minutes.

Bake in 350° oven 35 to 40 minutes or until done. Remove from pan; cool on rack. Makes 1 loaf.

BEAR CLAWS: Use ½ of Basic Sweet Dough. Combine ¾ c. chopped dates, ¼ c. water and ¼ c. brown sugar in saucepan. Cook over low heat, stirring occasionally, until thickened (about 10 minutes). Cool and add ½ c. chopped pecans.

Roll dough into 18x6-inch rectangle. Spread one half, lengthwise, with date filling. Fold over, pressing edges together. Cut in 2-inch pieces. Place on greased baking sheet. Make 2 or 3 cuts about 1-inch long in edge of dough opposite fold. Cover and let rise in warm place until doubled.

Bake in 350° oven 20 to 25 minutes or until done. Remove from baking sheets; cool on racks. Spread with your favorite confectioners sugar icing while still warm. Makes about 9 bear claws.

KOLACHES: Use ½ of Basic Sweet Dough. Roll to ¼-inch thickness and cut into 2-inch rounds. Place on greased baking sheets. Cover and let rise in warm place until doubled.

Combine ¾ c. chopped cooked prunes, 2 tblsp. prune juice, ¼ c. sugar, 1½ tsp. lemon juice, ¼ tsp. ground cinnamon and ⅛ tsp. ground cloves in bowl; mix well. Make a hollow in center of each kolache with thumb. Brush kolache with melted butter. Fill hollows with prune filling.

Bake in 350° oven 20 to 25 minutes or until done. Remove from baking sheets; cool on racks. Sprinkle with confectioners sugar. Makes about 18 kolaches.

BUBBLE RING: Use ½ of Basic Sweet Dough. Form dough into 2 rolls, about 10 inches long. Cut each roll into 10 pieces. Form each piece into 2 small balls. Place layer of balls about ½-inch apart in well-greased 10-inch tube pan. Brush with melted butter. Sprinkle with chopped nuts. Arrange 2 more layers, placing balls over spaces in each layer below and using about ½ c. chopped nuts in all.

Combine ⅓ c. dark corn syrup, 2 tblsp. melted butter and ½ tsp. vanilla in bowl; pour over ring. Cover and let rise in warm place until doubled, about 45 minutes.

Bake in 350° oven 35 to 40 minutes. Let stand in pan about 5 minutes before turning out onto plate. Makes 1 Bubble Ring.

CINNAMON PUFFS

> 1 pkg. active dry yeast
> ½ c. warm water (115°F.)
> ½ c. milk, scalded
> ¼ c. shortening
> 1 tblsp. sugar
> 1 tsp. salt
> 2 eggs
> 3 c. sifted flour
> ¼ c. butter, melted
> 2 tblsp. butter, melted
> ¾ tsp. ground cinnamon
> ¼ c. sugar

Sprinkle yeast over warm water; stir to dissolve. Combine milk, shortening, 1 tblsp. sugar and salt in mixing bowl. Cool to lukewarm. Add eggs, yeast mixture and flour. Beat at medium speed of electric mixer 2 minutes. *Do not knead.* Brush surface of dough with oil. Cover and let rise in warm place until doubled, about 1 hour.

Stir dough four or five times with spoon. Dip spoon in the ¼ c. melted butter before spooning dough into well-greased muffin-pan cups. Cover and let rise in warm place until doubled.

Bake in 375° oven 15 to 20 minutes. Remove from pan. While still warm, dip top of each muffin in 2 tblsp. melted butter, then in combined cinnamon and ¼ c. sugar. Makes 24 muffins.

REFRIGERATOR ROLLS

1 pkg. active dry yeast
1 c. warm water (115° F.)
½ c. butter, melted and cooled
3 eggs, well beaten
4½ c. unsifted flour
½ c. sugar
1 tsp. salt

Sprinkle yeast over warm water; stir to dissolve. Combine butter, eggs and yeast mixture in mixing bowl. Combine flour, sugar and salt. Beat dry ingredients into yeast mixture. Add a little more flour, if necessary, to make a soft dough. *Do not knead.* Cover and refrigerate 1½ hours or more.

Remove dough from refrigerator. Let stand at room temperature 30 minutes for easier handling. Shape as desired. Place on greased baking sheets or in baking pans. Cover and let rise in warm place until doubled.

Bake in 425° oven 12 to 15 minutes or until done. Remove from sheets; cool on racks. Makes 24 rolls.

WHOLE WHEAT SANDWICH BUNS

2 c. water
½ c. sugar
½ c. nonfat dry milk
1 tblsp. salt
¾ c. cooking oil
4½ to 5 c. sifted flour
2 pkgs. active dry yeast
3 eggs
3½ c. stirred whole wheat flour
Milk

Combine water, sugar, dry milk, salt and cooking oil in saucepan. Heat to very warm (120-130° F.). Stir together 4 c. flour and yeast in bowl. Add warm liquid and eggs. Beat at low speed of electric mixer ½ minute, scraping sides and bottom of bowl constantly. Beat at high speed 3 minutes, scraping bowl occasionally. Stir in whole wheat flour by hand. Add enough remaining flour to make a moderately soft dough. Knead on floured surface until smooth and elastic, about 5 minutes. Place in greased bowl, turning to grease top. Cover and let rise until doubled, about 1½ hours.

Punch down dough. Divide in thirds. Cover and let rest 5 minutes. Divide each third into 8 portions. Shape into balls. Place on greased baking sheets. Press down each with palm of hand to make 3½-inch rounds. Cover and let rise until doubled, 30 to 45 minutes. Brush with milk.

Bake in 375° oven 12 minutes or until golden brown. Remove from sheets; cool on racks. Makes 24 buns.

KAFFEE KUCHEN RING

1 pkg. active dry yeast
1 c. warm milk (115°F.)
3½ c. sifted flour
1 c. sugar
½ c. butter
4 eggs
¼ tsp. ground nutmeg
1 tsp. grated lemon rind
¾ tsp. salt
Blanched whole almonds

Soften yeast in warm milk in small bowl. Stir in 1 c. flour and 1 tsp. of the sugar. Beat well. Cover and let rise in warm place until bubbly, about 15 minutes.

Generously butter 10-inch fluted tube pan. Arrange almonds in design in bottom.

Cream together butter and remaining sugar in mixing bowl until light and fluffy. Add eggs, one at a time, beating well after each addition. Beat in nutmeg and lemon rind. Blend in yeast mixture. Mix in remaining flour and salt; beat well. Turn into prepared fluted tube pan. Cover and let rise in warm place until doubled, about 1¼ hours.

Bake in 350° oven 40 to 45 minutes or until done. Cool on rack 10 minutes. Remove from pan; cool on rack. Makes 1 coffee cake.

SQUASH ROLLS

½ c. milk
¼ c. sugar
1 tsp. salt
¼ c. shortening
½ c. mashed cooked Hubbard squash
1 pkg. active dry yeast
¼ c. warm water (115°F.)
3 to 3¼ c. unsifted flour

Heat together milk, sugar, salt and shortening in saucepan until warm (115°F.). Stir in squash. Soften yeast in warm water. Beat half the flour into milk mixture. Stir in softened yeast. Beat well. Mix in enough flour to make a soft dough.

Turn out on lightly floured surface and knead until smooth and satiny, about 8 to 10 minutes. Place dough in lightly greased bowl, turning dough once to grease surface. Cover and let rise in warm place until doubled, about 45 minutes.

Punch down dough. Shape in rolls as desired. Place on greased baking sheets. Cover and let rise in warm place until doubled, about 45 minutes.

Bake in 400° oven 10 minutes or until done. Remove from baking sheets; cool on racks. Makes 24 rolls.

"PLUM LUSCIOUS" COFFEE CAKE

2 c. unsifted flour
3 tsp baking powder
1 tsp. salt
⅓ c. sugar
¼ c. lard
2 tblsp. butter, softened
2 eggs
½ c. milk (about)
6 or 8 red or blue plums, quartered
2 tblsp. butter
1 c. brown sugar, firmly packed
1½ tsp. ground cinnamon

Sift together flour, baking powder, salt and sugar into mixing bowl. Cut in lard and 2 tblsp. butter with pastry blender or two knives until mixture resembles coarse meal. Beat eggs slightly in measuring cup. Add enough milk to eggs to make 1 c. Add to flour mixture; stir just until moistened.

Turn mixture into greased 11x7x1½-inch baking dish, spreading dough evenly into corners of pan. Press plums into dough and dot with the 2 tblsp. butter. Combine brown sugar and cinnamon; sprinkle over plums.

Bake in 375° oven 20 to 25 minutes or until done. Cool on rack. Serve warm. Makes 1 coffee cake.

SUGAR-COCONUT TWISTS

2 c. unsifted flour
3 tsp. baking powder
1 tsp. salt
2 tblsp. sugar
¼ c. lard
2 tblsp. butter, softened
2 eggs
¼ c. milk (about)
2 tblsp. butter, softened
½ c. brown sugar, firmly packed
½ c. flaked coconut

Sift together flour, baking powder, salt and sugar into mixing bowl. Cut in lard and 2 tblsp. butter with pastry blender or two knives until mixture resembles coarse meal. Beat eggs slightly in measuring cup. Add enough milk to eggs to make ¾ c. Add to flour mixture; stir just until moistened. Turn out on lightly floured surface and knead gently about 30 seconds.

Roll dough in 8x12-inch rectangle. Spread with the 2 tblsp. softened butter along one lengthwise half. Lightly sprinkle with brown sugar and coconut. Fold other half of dough over filling and press edges to seal. Cut in strips 1 inch wide and twist, pinching ends together. Place on greased baking sheet.

Bake in 425° oven 10 to 12 minutes or until golden brown. Remove from baking sheets; serve warm. Makes 1 dozen rolls.

APRICOT-BRAN MUFFINS

2 c. unsifted flour
4½ tsp. baking powder
1 tsp. salt
½ c. sugar
1½ c. milk
2 c. whole bran
2 eggs
½ c. butter, melted
½ c. finely cut dried apricots

Sift together flour, baking powder, salt and sugar. Pour milk over bran in mixing bowl and let stand until most of milk is absorbed. Beat in eggs. Stir in melted butter and apricots. Add sifted dry ingredients; stir just enough to moisten. Spoon in greased or paper-lined muffin-pan cups.

Bake in 400° oven 25 to 30 minutes or until golden brown. Makes 18 muffins.

CORNMEAL SURPRISE MUFFINS

1 c. sifted flour
1 c. cornmeal
2 tblsp. sugar
3 tsp. baking powder
½ tsp. salt
1 egg, beaten
1 c. milk
3 tblsp. cooking oil
Red raspberry or currant jelly

Sift together flour, cornmeal, sugar, baking powder and salt into mixing bowl.

Combine egg, milk and oil in another bowl; beat to blend. Add to dry ingredients, stirring just enough to moisten. Spoon batter into 10 greased 3-inch muffin-pan cups, filling one-half full. Place scant teaspoonful of red raspberry jelly in each. Top with enough batter to fill two-thirds full.

Bake in 425° oven 20 minutes or until golden. Makes 10 muffins.

SPICED APPLE MUFFINS

2 c. sifted flour
3 tsp. baking powder
½ tsp. salt
½ tsp. ground cinnamon
¼ c. sugar
¼ c. soft shortening
1 egg, slightly beaten
1 c. milk
1 c. finely chopped red apples
⅓ c. brown sugar, firmly packed
⅓ c. finely chopped walnuts
½ tsp. ground cinnamon

Sift together flour, baking powder, salt, ½ tsp. cinnamon and sugar into mixing bowl. Cut in shortening with pastry blender or two knives until mixture resembles coarse meal. Combine egg and milk; add with apple to flour mixture, stirring lightly until just blended. Fill greased 2½-inch muffin-pan cups two-thirds full. Combine brown sugar, walnuts and ½ tsp. cinnamon; sprinkle on top.

Bake in 400° oven 20 to 25 minutes or until done. Remove from pans. Makes 12 muffins.

QUICK COFFEE RING

2 c. sifted flour
3 tsp. baking powder
1 tsp. salt
2 tblsp. sugar
6 tblsp. butter
1 egg
½ c. milk (about)
¼ c. butter, softened
½ c. brown sugar, firmly packed
1 tblsp. ground cinnamon
1 tsp. ground allspice
½ c. raisins
½ c. chopped walnuts

Sift together flour, baking powder, salt and sugar into mixing bowl. Cut in 6 tblsp. butter with pastry blender or two knives until mixture resembles coarse meal. Beat egg slightly in measuring cup. Add enough milk to egg to make ¾ c. Add all at once to flour mixture, stirring only enough to moisten dry ingredients. Turn onto lightly floured surface. Knead gently about 30 seconds. Roll into 12x9-inch rectangle. Spread with ¼ c. softened butter.

Combine brown sugar, cinnamon, allspice, raisins and walnuts. Sprinkle over dough to about 1 inch from edges. Roll as for jelly roll from 9-inch side. Place, sealed edge down, to form ring on greased baking sheet. Cut through ring almost to center at 1-inch intervals with scissors. Turn each slice slightly on its side.

Bake in 425° oven 15 to 20 minutes or until evenly browned. While ring is still warm, ice with your favorite confectioners sugar frosting. Remove from baking sheet; serve warm. Makes 1 coffee ring.

CRANBERRY-ORANGE BREAD

2 c. sifted flour
1 c. sugar
1½ tsp. baking powder
½ tsp. baking soda
½ tsp. salt
1 egg, slightly beaten
2 tblsp. melted butter
½ c. orange juice
2 tblsp. hot water
½ c. chopped walnuts
1 c. coarsely cut cranberries
2 tsp. grated orange rind

Sift together flour, sugar, baking powder, baking soda and salt into mixing bowl. Add egg, butter, orange juice and water; mix only until ingredients are moistened. Fold in walnuts, cranberries and orange rind. Pour batter into greased 9x5x3-inch loaf pan. Allow to stand for 20 minutes at room temperature.

Bake in 350° oven about 1 hour or until done. Remove from pan; cool on rack. For easier slicing, wrap and store in cool place for 24 hours before cutting. Makes 1 loaf.

DATE WHIRLS

1¼ c. chopped dates
½ c. water
½ c. sugar
1 tblsp. lemon juice
¼ c. chopped walnuts
2¼ c. sifted flour
½ tsp. baking soda
½ tsp. salt
½ c. butter
1 c. brown sugar, firmly packed
1 egg
1 tsp. lemon juice
½ tsp. vanilla

Combine dates, water, sugar and 1 tblsp. lemon juice in small saucepan. Cook over low heat, stirring occasionally, until mixture is thickened. Remove from heat; cool. Stir in walnuts.

Sift together flour, baking soda and salt.

Cream together butter and brown sugar in mixing bowl until light and fluffy. Beat in egg. Stir in 1 tsp. lemon juice and vanilla. Add dry ingredients and mix well. Cover and chill dough thoroughly.

Divide dough in half. Roll each portion into rectangle about ¼ inch thick on floured surface. Spread with half of Date Filling. Roll as for jelly roll, from wide side, sealing edges. Wrap in waxed paper and refrigerate until well chilled.

Cut rolls into thin slices. Place on ungreased baking sheets, about 2 inches apart.

Bake in 400° oven 8 to 10 minutes or until done. Remove from baking sheets; cool on racks. Makes about 4 dozen cookies.

VANILLA BUTTER THINS

2¼ c. unsifted flour
1 tsp. baking soda
1 tsp. cream of tartar
⅛ tsp. salt
1 c. butter
1¼ c. unsifted confectioners sugar
1 egg
1 tsp. vanilla

Sift together flour, baking soda, cream of tartar and salt.

Cream together butter and confectioners sugar in mixing bowl until light and fluffy. Beat in egg and vanilla. Add sifted dry ingredients and mix well. Shape dough in two rolls about 2 inches in diameter. Wrap in waxed paper and chill thoroughly.

Cut roll in slices about ¼ inch thick with sharp knife. Place on ungreased baking sheets.

Bake in 375° oven 8 to 10 minutes or until golden brown. Remove from baking sheets; cool on racks. Makes about 5 dozen cookies.

Variation: Trim cookies before baking by pressing a chocolate chip or a pecan half in the center of each.

BUTTERSCOTCH SLICES

1¾ c. sifted flour
½ tsp. baking powder
⅛ tsp. salt
½ c. butter
1 c. brown sugar, firmly packed
1 egg
½ c. finely chopped walnuts

Sift together flour, baking powder and salt.

Cream together butter and sugar in mixing bowl until light and fluffy. Beat in egg. Add dry ingredients and mix well. Add walnuts, mixing to distribute evenly through dough.

Shape dough in two rolls, about 2 inches in diameter. Wrap in waxed paper. Refrigerate until firm, at least several hours.

Cut rolls into ¼-inch slices with sharp knife. Place on ungreased baking sheets.

Bake in 375° oven 8 to 10 minutes or until lightly browned. Remove from baking sheets; cool on racks. Makes about 7 dozen cookies.

CHOCOLATE PECAN CRISPIES

1 c. sifted flour
1 c. sugar
½ tsp. baking soda
½ tsp. salt
½ c. soft shortening
1 egg
1 tsp. vanilla
2 (1 oz.) squares unsweetened chocolate,
    melted and cooled slightly
1 c. quick-cooking rolled oats
½ c. chopped pecans

Sift together flour, sugar, baking soda and salt into mixing bowl. Add shortening, egg, vanilla and chocolate. Blend until smooth, about 2 minutes. (Dough will be stiff.) Mix in oats and pecans. Drop dough by teaspoonfuls onto ungreased baking sheets. Flatten with floured tines of fork.

Bake in 350° oven 12 to 14 minutes or until done. Remove from baking sheets; cool on racks. Makes 3½ to 4 dozen cookies.

FROSTED APPLESAUCE NUT DROPS

2 c. unsifted flour
½ tsp. salt
½ tsp. baking soda
½ tsp. ground nutmeg
½ tsp. ground cinnamon
½ c. butter
1 c. brown sugar, firmly packed
2 eggs
½ tsp. vanilla
⅔ c. applesauce
½ c. chopped walnuts
1½ c. sifted confectioners sugar
1 tblsp. soft butter
¼ tsp. vanilla
2 tsp. light cream (about)

Sift together flour, salt, baking soda, nutmeg and cinnamon.

Cream together ½ c. butter and brown sugar in mixing bowl until light and fluffy. Beat in eggs and ½ tsp. vanilla. Add dry ingredients alternately with applesauce, beginning and ending with dry ingredients. Beat until smooth after each addition. Stir in walnuts. Cover and chill dough.

Drop by teaspoonfuls, about 2 inches apart, on lightly greased baking sheets.

Bake in 375° oven 10 to 12 minutes or until lightly browned. Remove from baking sheets; cool on racks.

When cool, frost lightly with icing. Blend together confectioners sugar and 1 tblsp. butter in bowl. Beat in ¼ tsp. vanilla and enough cream to make frosting of spreading consistency. Makes 6 dozen cookies.

RAGGEDY ANNS

3 c. unsifted flour
1 tsp. baking soda
1 c. butter
¾ c. sugar
1½ c. brown sugar, firmly packed
2 eggs
½ c. flaked coconut
1 c. Spanish peanuts

Combine flour and baking soda.

Cream together butter and sugars in mixing bowl until light and fluffy. Beat in eggs. Blend in flour mixture. Stir in coconut and peanuts. Drop by teaspoonfuls onto ungreased baking sheets.

Bake in 375° oven 10 to 12 minutes or until golden. Remove from baking sheets; cool on racks. Makes 7 dozen cookies.

NUTTY BROWNIE MOUNDS

1 c . unsifted flour
½ tsp. salt
½ tsp. baking powder
½ c. butter
1 c. sugar
2 eggs
1½ tsp. vanilla
2 (1 oz.) squares unsweetened chocolate,
    melted and cooled
1 c. coarsely chopped walnuts

Sift together flour, salt and baking powder.

Cream together butter and sugar in mixing bowl until light and fluffy. Beat in eggs and vanilla. Blend in chocolate. Add dry ingredients and mix well. Stir in walnuts. Drop by teaspoonfuls onto lightly greased baking sheets.

Bake in 350° oven 10 to 12 minutes or until done. Remove from baking sheets; cool on racks. Makes about 4½ dozen cookies.

AMBROSIA DROPS

1¼ c. sifted flour
½ tsp. baking powder
½ tsp. salt
½ c. butter
½ c. sugar
1 egg
1 tsp. grated orange rind
1 c. coarsely chopped walnuts
1 c. flaked coconut
Halved walnuts

Sift together flour, baking powder and salt.

Cream together butter and sugar in mixing bowl until light and fluffy. Add egg and beat well. Mix in dry ingredients. Add orange rind, walnuts and coconut; mix well. Drop by teaspoonfuls onto ungreased baking sheets. Press walnut half into center of each cookie.

Bake in 375° oven 12 to 14 minutes until lightly browned. Remove from baking sheets; cool on racks. Makes 3 dozen cookies.

CHOCOLATE BROWNIES

½ c. butter
2 (1 oz.) squares unsweetened chocolate
2 eggs
1 c. sugar
½ tsp. vanilla
½ c. unsifted flour
½ c. chopped walnuts

Melt together butter and chocolate in saucepan. Cool slightly. Beat eggs slightly in bowl. Blend in sugar and vanilla. Combine chocolate mixture with egg mixture. Stir in flour. Pour batter into greased 11x7x1½-inch baking dish. Sprinkle with walnuts.

Bake in 350° oven 35 to 40 minutes or until done. Cool in pan on rack. Cut into bars while still warm. Makes about 20 cookies.

SOUR CREAM DROPS

2 c. unsifted flour
2 tsp. baking powder
¾ tsp. salt
½ tsp. baking soda
½ tsp. ground nutmeg
½ c. butter
1 c. brown sugar, firmly packed
1 egg
½ c. dairy sour cream
½ c. chopped walnuts

Sift together flour, baking powder, salt, baking soda and nutmeg.

Cream together butter and brown sugar in mixing bowl until light and fluffy. Beat in egg. Add dry ingredients alternately with sour cream, beating until smooth after each addition. Stir in walnuts. Drop by teaspoonfuls onto ungreased baking sheets.

Bake in 400° oven 8 to 10 minutes or until done. Remove from baking sheets; cool on racks. Makes 6 dozen cookies.

DATE-NUT ROCKS

    1¾ c. unsifted flour
    ½ tsp. baking soda
    ½ tsp. salt
    ½ tsp. ground nutmeg
    ½ tsp. ground cinnamon
    ½ c. butter
    1 c. brown sugar, firmly packed
    1 egg
    ¼ c. cold coffee
    1 c. cut-up dates
    ½ c. chopped walnuts

Sift together flour, baking soda, salt, nutmeg and cinnamon.

Cream together butter and sugar in mixing bowl until light and fluffy. Beat in egg. Add dry ingredients alternately with coffee, beating well after each addition. Stir in dates and walnuts. Cover and chill dough. Drop by teaspoonfuls onto ungreased baking sheets.

Bake in 375° oven 8 to 10 minutes or until done. Remove from baking sheets; cool on racks. Makes 4 dozen cookies.

FROSTED MINCEMEAT BARS

1 c. sifted flour
1½ tsp. baking powder
1 tsp. salt
¼ c. butter
1 c. sugar
2 eggs
1 c. prepared mincemeat
2 tsp. grated orange rind
½ c. chopped walnuts
Confectioners Sugar Icing
   (recipe follows)

Sift together flour, baking powder and salt.

Cream together butter and sugar in mixing bowl until light and fluffy. Beat in eggs, one at a time, beating well after each addition. Stir in dry ingredients. Stir in mincemeat, orange rind and walnuts. Spread batter in greased 11x7x1½-inch baking dish.

Bake in 325° oven 35 minutes or until done. Cool in pan on rack. Frost with Confectioners Sugar Icing. Cut in bars. Makes 24.

Confectioners Sugar Icing: Combine 3 c. sifted confectioners sugar, 3 tblsp. orange juice and 1 tsp. grated orange rind in bowl; mix until smooth.

TOFFEE BARS

1 c. butter
1 c. brown sugar, firmly packed
1 egg
1 tsp. rum flavoring
2 c. unsifted flour
¼ tsp. salt
1 (6 oz.) pkg. semi-sweet chocolate
    pieces, melted
½ c. finely chopped walnuts

Cream together butter and brown sugar in mixing bowl until light and fluffy. Beat in egg and rum flavoring. Stir in flour and salt; mix well. Spread dough in ungreased 15½x10½x1-inch jelly roll pan.

Bake in 325° oven 20 to 25 minutes or until evenly browned. Cool in pan on rack. While still warm, spread with melted chocolate and sprinkle with nuts. Cut in diamond-shaped bars. Makes about 4 dozen cookies.

PENUCHE BARS

1 c. sifted flour
1 tsp. baking powder
¼ tsp. salt
¼ c. butter
1 c. brown sugar, firmly packed
1 egg
½ tsp. vanilla
1 (6 oz.) pkg. semi-sweet chocolate
   or butterscotch pieces
½ c. chopped walnuts

Sift together flour, baking powder and salt.

Melt butter in saucepan. Beat in brown sugar. Cool slightly. Add egg and vanilla. Beat until mixture is light. Stir in dry ingredients. Gently stir in chocolate or butterscotch pieces and walnuts. Spread mixture evenly in greased 8-inch square baking pan.

Bake in 350° oven 25 to 30 minutes or until done. Cool in pan on rack. Cut in 2x1-inch bars. Makes 32 cookies.

CHINESE ALMOND COOKIES

3 c. sifted flour
1 tsp. baking powder
½ tsp. salt
½ c. lard
½ c. butter
1 c. sugar
3 egg yolks
1½ tsp. almond extract
1 egg white, beaten
Blanched whole almonds

Sift together flour, baking powder and salt. Cream together lard and butter in mixing bowl. Gradually add sugar and beat until light and fluffy. Beat in egg yolks and almond extract. Add flour mixture, mixing well to form dough. (It will be crumbly.)

Shape dough into 1-inch balls and place about 2 inches apart on greased baking sheets. With bottom of glass, flatten to ½-inch thickness. Dip almonds in egg white and press one in center of each cookie.

Bake in 375° oven 10 to 12 minutes or until golden. Remove from baking sheets; cool on racks. Makes 5½ dozen cookies.

PRALINE COOKIES

1¼ c. unsifted flour
¼ tsp. salt
½ c. butter
1½ c. brown sugar, firmly packed
1 egg
1 tsp. vanilla
1 c. coarsely chopped pecans

Combine flour and salt.

Cream together butter and brown sugar in mixing bowl until light and fluffy. Beat in egg and vanilla. Add flour mixture and mix well. Stir in pecans. Cover and chill dough.

Shape dough in balls about 1 inch in diameter. Place on lightly greased baking sheets. With bottom of glass, flatten each ball to about ¼-inch thickness.

Bake in 375° oven 8 to 10 minutes or until done. Cool on baking sheets about 2 minutes; remove and cool completely on racks. Makes about 3 dozen cookies.

SCOTCH SHORTBREAD

1 c. butter
½ c. sugar
2 c. sifted flour

Cream together butter and sugar in mixing bowl until light and fluffy. Blend in flour thoroughly. Cover and chill.

Roll chilled dough out on floured surface to ¼-inch thickness. Cut into desired shapes. Place on ungreased baking sheets.

Bake in 300° oven 20 to 25 minutes or until firm but not browned. Remove from baking sheets; cool on racks. Makes 4 to 5 dozen cookies.

TOASTED ALMOND FINGERS

---

1 c. butter
½ c. unsifted confectioners sugar
1 tblsp. light cream
1 tsp. vanilla
2 c. sifted flour
¼ tsp. salt
1 c. finely chopped toasted almonds
2 tblsp. soft butter
1 c. sifted confectioners sugar
2 tblsp. baking cocoa
1 tblsp. cold coffee

Cream together 1 c. butter and ½ c. confectioners sugar in mixing bowl until light and fluffy. Beat in cream and vanilla. Add flour and salt, mixing to form a soft dough. Stir in almonds. Cover and chill dough thoroughly.

Shape chilled dough into "fingers" and place on ungreased baking sheets.

Bake in 325° oven about 15 minutes or until delicately browned. Remove from baking sheets; cool on racks.

Combine 2 tblsp. butter, 1 c. confectioners sugar, cocoa and coffee in bowl; blend well. Dip one end of each cooled cookie into frosting. Place on cooling racks to set frosting. Makes 6 dozen cookies.

CINNAMON-NUT DISCS

> 1¼ c. unsifted flour
> 1 tsp. baking powder
> ¼ tsp. salt
> ½ c. butter
> 1 c. sugar
> 1 egg
> 1 tsp. vanilla
> ½ c. finely chopped walnuts
> 2 tsp. ground cinnamon

Sift together flour, baking powder and salt.

Cream together butter and sugar in mixing bowl until light and fluffy. Beat in egg and vanilla. Mix in dry ingredients. Cover and chill dough thoroughly.

Shape dough into small balls, using about 1 teaspoonful for each. Roll in mixture of walnuts and cinnamon. Place about 2 inches apart on ungreased baking sheets.

Bake in 375° oven 12 to 15 minutes or until done. Remove from baking sheets immediately; cool on racks. Makes 2½ to 3 dozen cookies.

ORANGE SANDWICH COOKIES

1½ c. sifted flour
¼ tsp. baking soda
½ tsp. salt
½ c. butter
½ c. sugar
1 egg
½ tsp. vanilla
1 tsp. grated orange rind
½ c. finely chopped walnuts
Orange Marmalade Frosting
(recipe follows)

Sift together flour, baking soda and salt.

Cream together butter and sugar in mixing bowl until light and fluffy. Beat in egg. Stir in vanilla and orange rind. Mix in dry ingredients. Stir in walnuts. Cover and chill dough thoroughly.

Roll chilled dough out on floured surface. Cut with 1¾-inch round cookie cutter. Place on ungreased baking sheets.

Bake in 400° oven 8 to 10 minutes or until lightly browned. Remove at once to cooling racks.

When cookies are cool, frost half of them with Orange Marmalade Frosting. Top with remaining cookies to form "sandwiches." Makes about 2 dozen sandwich cookies.

Orange Marmalade Frosting: Combine 2¼ c. sifted confectioners sugar, ¼ c. soft butter and ½ c. orange marmalade in bowl; beat until smooth and creamy.

CHAPTER VIII

Scrumptious
Fix-Ahead Desserts

The fix-ahead approach is ideal for desserts, whether you're making a simple family pudding or a company spectacular. When you're planning to use the oven to bake, why not whip up a cake or make a batch of tart shells to utilize the empty space on the oven rack. Or, you can organize a "bake-in" morning (see Chapter VII) and prepare a number of desserts to freeze for later use.

Unfrosted cakes—butter, pound, angel, chiffon, sponge—hold very well in the freezer for up to 6 months. Since they thaw quickly, you can use them in limitless ways..Top plain cake with fruit, sauce or ice cream. Create glamorous desserts by cutting cake into layers; fill with with ice cream, fillings or whipped cream, then frost and decorate.

If you wish to frost and freeze cakes, use an uncooked confectioners sugar frosting and freeze before wrapping. Then wrap securely. These cakes will retain quality 2 to 3 months in storage.

Pastry-type desserts give you many options. Pies, shells, rounds or squares can all be frozen either unbaked or baked. However, unbaked fruit pies, frozen and baked later, usually have a fuller fruit flavor, a crisper, more tender crust. Besides, reheating frozen baked pies takes almost as much time as the original baking, so you are spending exta oven energy.

Many desserts are very fragile and need special handling. Package them in rigid plastic or metal containers or cardboard cartons to prevent crushing or shattering. Use foil pie pans as lids to protect tender crusts before wrapping pies for the freezer.

PERFECT PASTRY FOR 1-CRUST PIE

> 1½ c. unsifted flour
> ¾ tsp. salt
> ½ c. lard
> 2½ tblsp. water

Combine flour and salt in mixing bowl. Cut in lard with pastry blender or two knives until mixture resembles coarse meal. Sprinkle water over mixture. Lightly mix with fork or fingers until dough just holds together. Form dough into a ball. Place on lightly floured surface.

Roll dough lightly from center to edges using floured stockinette-covered rolling pin. Roll to ⅛-inch thickness. Fold in half and place in 9-inch pie pan. Place evenly in pie pan and do not stretch dough. Trim about 1 inch from rim of pie pan. Form rim around edge of pan. Flute edge. Prick pastry with fork.

Bake in 450° oven 10 to 15 minutes or until golden brown. Cool on rack. Makes 1 (9-inch) pie shell.

To Freeze: Do not prick pie shell with fork. Wrap in aluminum foil and freeze.

To Bake: Place unwrapped frozen pie shell in 475° oven. After 2 minutes, prick pastry with fork. Continue baking 6 to 8 more minutes or until golden brown.

PERFECT PASTRY FOR 2-CRUST PIE

2 c. unsifted flour
1 tsp. salt
⅔ c. lard
¼ c. water

Combine flour and salt in mixing bowl. Cut in lard with pastry blender or two knives until mixture resembles coarse meal. Sprinkle water over mixture. Lightly mix with fork or fingers until dough just holds together. Form dough into a ball. Divide almost in half. Place larger half on lightly floured surface.

Roll dough lightly from center to edges using floured stockinette-covered rolling pin. Roll to ⅛-inch thickness. Fold in half and place in 9-inch pie pan. Fit dough in pie pan being careful not to stretch dough. Arrange filling in pie crust.

Roll out remaining dough about ½ inch larger than diameter of pie. Place over filling. Tuck under edge of bottom crust. Crimp or flute edges. If you wish to bake immediately, cut vents. (Do not cut vents in pie if you wish to freeze it.) Follow baking directions for pie. Makes 1 (2-crust) 9-inch pie.

To Freeze: Freeze unbaked pie until firm. Remove and wrap in aluminum foil. Label and freeze.

To Bake: Remove wrapping. Place a strip of aluminum foil around rim of pie to prevent over-browning. Bake on lower shelf of 425° oven 15 to 20 minutes longer than regular baking time. Cut vents in top crust after pie has been in oven about 10 minutes.

Note: Baked 2-crust pies can also be frozen. To serve, let stand at room temperature about 30 minutes. Unwrap and bake on lower shelf of 350° oven 30 to 40 minutes or until warm.

PERFECT PASTRY MIX

---

6 c. unsifted flour
3 tsp. salt
2 c. lard (1 lb.)

Combine flour and salt in large mixing bowl. Cut in lard with pastry blender or two knives until mixture resembles coarse meal. Cover tightly. Store mix in refrigerator for up to one month. Makes about 8 cups.

To Use Mix: Lightly spoon dry pastry mix into measuring cup. Do not sift. Add water and proceed as for regular pastry.
For 1-crust pie: 2 c. Pastry Mix plus 2½ tblsp. water
For 2-crust pie: 2⅔ c. Pastry Mix plus ¼ c. water
For 6 to 8 tart shells: Same as 2-crust pie. Bake frozen unbaked tart shells in 425° oven 8 to 10 minutes. Prick with fork after 2 minutes in oven. Frozen baked tart shells can be reheated in 325° oven 6 to 8 minutes.

OLD-FASHIONED APPLE PIE

Pastry for 2-crust pie
¾ c. sugar
2 tblsp. flour
½ tsp. ground cinnamon
⅛ tsp. salt
6 c. sliced tart apples (6 or 7)
    or 2 (1 lb. 4 oz.) cans
    pie-sliced apples, drained
2 tblsp. butter

Make pastry. Before adding water, set aside ¼ c. of the flour-lard mixture.

Fit bottom crust into 9-inch pie pan.

Combine sugar, flour, cinnamon and salt in bowl. Sprinkle 2 tblsp. of mixture over bottom crust. Combine remaining mixture with apples; turn into crust.

Dot apples with butter. Fit on top crust, trim and crimp edges to seal. Cut vents to allow steam to escape if baking immediately. Sprinkle ¼ c. reserved flour-lard mixture over top.

Bake in 425° oven 35 to 40 minutes or until top is browned and apples are tender. Makes 1 (9-inch) pie.

To Freeze Unbaked Pie: Do not cut vents in top crust. Freeze pie until firm. Remove and wrap in aluminum foil. Label and freeze.

To Bake: Remove wrapping. Place a strip of aluminum foil around rim of pie to prevent over-browning. Bake on lower shelf of 425° oven 50 to 60 minutes or until top is browned and apples are tender.

ORANGE MINCEMEAT PIE

Pastry for 2-Crust pie
4 c. prepared mincemeat
2 tsp. grated orange rind
⅓ c. orange juice

Make pastry. Fit bottom crust into 9-inch pie pan.

Combine mincemeat, orange rind and orange juice. Turn into crust. Fit on top crust, trim and crimp edges to seal. With star-shaped cookie cutter, gently press in about 5 places on crust to make vents if baking immediately.

Bake in 425° oven 25 to 30 minutes or until top is browned. Makes 1 (9-inch) pie.

To Freeze Unbaked Pie: Do not cut vents in top crust. Freeze pie until firm. Remove and wrap in aluminum foil. Label and freeze.

To Bake: Remove wrapping. Place a strip of aluminum foil around rim of pie to prevent over-browning. Bake on lower shelf of 425° oven 40 to 50 minutes or until top is browned.

BLUEBERRY PIE WITH LEMON CRUST

2 c. unsifted flour
1 tsp. salt
¼ c. sugar
1 tsp. grated lemon rind
⅔ c. lard
3 tblsp. lemon juice
1 tblsp. water
1 c. sugar
5 tblsp. flour
⅛ tsp. salt
4 c. fresh blueberries
2 tblsp. butter

Combine 2 c. flour, 1 tsp. salt, ¼ c. sugar and lemon rind in bowl. Cut in lard with pastry blender or two knives until mixture resembles coarse meal. Combine lemon juice and water; sprinkle over mixture. Lightly mix with fork until dough just holds together. Fit bottom crust into 9-inch pie pan.

Mix 1 c. sugar, 5 tblsp. flour and ⅛ tsp. salt in bowl; toss lightly with blueberries. Turn into crust and dot with butter. Fit on top crust, trim and crimp or flute edges to seal. Cut steam vents if baking immediately.

Bake in 425° oven 35 minutes. Makes 1 (9-inch) pie.

To Freeze Unbaked Pie: Do not cut vents in top crust. Freeze pie until firm. Remove and wrap in aluminum foil. Label and freeze.

To Bake: Remove wrapping. Place a strip of aluminum foil around rim of pie to prevent over-browning. Bake on lower shelf of 425° oven 45 to 60 minutes or until golden brown.

STRAWBERRY-RHUBARB PIE

Pastry for 2-crust pie
2 c. halved strawberries
2 c. diced, fresh rhubarb, 1-inch pieces
1½ c. sugar
¼ c. quick-cooking tapioca
    or 6 tblsp. flour
⅛ tsp. salt
1 tsp. grated orange rind
2 tblsp. butter

Prepare pastry. Fit bottom crust into 9-inch pie pan.
Combine strawberries and rhubarb in large mixing bowl. Add sugar, tapioca, salt and orange rind. Toss gently until fruit is well-coated. Turn mixture into crust. Dot with butter. Fit with top crust. Trim and crimp edges to seal. Cut vents if baking immediately.

Bake in 425° oven 40 to 45 minutes or until top is browned. Makes 1 (9-inch) pie.

To Freeze Unbaked Pie: Do not cut vents in top crust. Freeze pie until firm. Remove and wrap in aluminum foil. Label and freeze.

To Bake: Remove wrapping. Place a strip of aluminum foil around rim of pie to prevent over-browning. Bake on lower shelf of 425° oven 55 to 65 minutes or until top is browned.

LIME CHIFFON PIE

1 env. unflavored gelatin
½ c. sugar
½ c. water
½ c. lime juice
4 egg yolks, slightly beaten
1 tsp. grated lime rind
4 egg whites
½ c. sugar
1 baked 9-inch pie shell
Whipped cream
Toasted coconut

Mix together gelatin and ½ c. sugar in top of double boiler. Combine water and lime juice; stir into beaten egg yolks. Add egg yolk mixture to gelatin-sugar mixture. Place over boiling water. Cook, stirring contantly, until gelatin is dissolved and mixture is slightly thickened, about 8 minutes. Stir in lime rind. Chill until mixture mounds slightly when dropped from spoon.

Beat egg whites in bowl until foamy. Gradually add ½ c. sugar, beating to make a stiff meringue. Fold lime mixture into meringue and pile into baked pie shell. Chill until set. Before serving, top with whipped cream and garnish with toasted coconut. Makes 1 (9-inch) pie.

To Freeze: Freeze pie until firm. Remove and wrap in aluminum foil carefully.

To Serve: Thaw in refrigerator about 3 hours or at room temperature about 45 minutes.

BAKED ALASKA CRANBERRY PIE

1 qt. vanilla ice cream, softened
1 baked 9-inch pie shell
3 egg whites
¼ tsp. cream of tartar
6 tblsp. sugar
1 (1 lb.) can jellied cranberry sauce

Spread ice cream evenly in bottom of baked pie shell. Freeze for 5 to 6 hours or overnight.

Beat egg whites and cream of tartar in bowl until soft peaks form. Gradually add sugar and beat until meringue is stiff and fine-textured.

Drain cranberry sauce. Cut sauce into slices and quickly arrange over ice cream in pie shell. Immediately spread meringue over cranberry sauce, bringing meringue to edges of crust to seal. Place pie on wooden cutting board in the oven.

Bake in 475° oven until meringue is golden brown, about 5 minutes. Serve at once. Makes 1 (9-inch) pie.

PEANUT BUTTER ICE CREAM PIE

1⅓ c. fine chocolate wafer crumbs
3 tblsp. melted butter
1 qt. vanilla ice cream
¾ c. crunchy peanut butter
½ c. heavy cream, whipped

Mix together chocolate wafer crumbs and melted butter in bowl. Press firmly into 9-inch pie pan.

Bake in 375° oven 8 minutes. Cool thoroughly.

Soften ice cream in bowl. Quickly blend in peanut butter. Then fold in whipped cream. Turn mixture into crust. Freeze until firm, about 5 to 6 hours. Temper in refrigerator about 15 minutes before serving. Makes 1 (9-inch) pie.

"TOP BANANA" CAKE

3¼ c. sifted cake flour
2 tsp. baking powder
¾ tsp. baking soda
¾ tsp. salt
1 c. butter
2 c. sugar
3 eggs
1½ c. mashed ripe bananas
½ c. buttermilk or sour milk
1½ tsp. vanilla
Fluffy Frosting (recipe follows)

Sift together cake flour, baking powder, baking soda and salt.

Cream together butter and sugar in mixing bowl until light and fluffy. Add eggs, one at a time, beating well after each addition.

Combine bananas, buttermilk and vanilla. Add banana mixture alternately with dry ingredients, beating until smooth after each addition. Pour batter into 3 greased and floured 9-inch round cake pans.

Bake in 350° oven 20 minutes or until cakes test done. Remove from pans; cool on racks. Frost with Fluffy Frosting. Makes 12 servings.

Fluffy Frosting: Combine 1 c. sugar, ⅓ c. water, ¼ tsp. cream of tartar and ⅛ tsp. salt in saucepan. Bring to a boil, stirring until sugar is dissolved. Add hot syrup very slowly to 2 egg whites in narrow mixing bowl. Beat with electric mixer at high speed 4 minutes or until stiff peaks are formed. Beat in 1 tsp. vanilla. Makes 4½ c. frosting.

ALMOND TOFFEE CAKE

> 2 c. sifted cake flour
> 3 tsp. baking powder
> ½ tsp. salt
> ½ c. butter
> 1 c. sugar
> 2 eggs
> ⅔ c. milk
> 1 tsp. vanilla
> Almond Toffee Frosting (recipe follows)
> Toasted slivered almonds

Sift together cake flour, baking powder and salt.

Cream together butter and sugar in mixing bowl until light and fluffy. Add eggs, one at a time, beating well after each addition. Add dry ingredients alternately with combined milk and vanilla, beating well after each addition. Pour batter into 2 greased and floured 8-inch round cake pans.

Bake in 350° oven about 25 minutes or until cake tests done. Cool in pans on racks 10 minutes. Remove from pans; cool on racks. Frost with Almond Toffee Frosting. Makes 12 servings.

Almond Toffee Frosting: Melt ½ c. butter in heavy saucepan. Heat, stirring constantly, until butter is deep golden brown. Remove from heat. Beat in 4½ c. sifted confectioners sugar, 1 tsp. vanilla and ¼ c. light cream. Add 2 or 3 tblsp. warm water. Continue beating until frosting is cool and of spreading consistency. Fill and frost tops and sides of layers. Wreathe top of cake with toasted slivered almonds.

CRUMB CAKE

---

3 c. sifted cake flour
2 c. brown sugar, firmly packed
½ tsp. salt
1 c. butter
1 tsp. baking soda
1 egg, slightly beaten
1 c. buttermilk or sour milk
½ c. chopped walnuts

Combine cake flour, brown sugar and salt in mixing bowl. Cut in butter with pastry blender or two knives, forming coarse crumbs. Reserve 1 c. crumbs for topping.

Add baking soda to combined egg and buttermilk. Add all at once to remaining crumb mixture; mix well. Pour batter into greased 13x9x2-inch baking pan. Combine chopped walnuts with reserved crumb mixture. Sprinkle over cake batter.

Bake in 375° oven about 35 minutes or until cake tests done. Cool in pan on rack. Makes 16 servings.

ITALIAN CREAM CAKE

12 eggs, separated
½ tsp. salt
1 tsp. cream of tartar
1⅓ c. sugar
1 tsp. vanilla
1⅓ c. sifted cake flour
Chocolate Spice Filling (recipe follows)
Lemon Fruit Filling (recipe follows)
1½ c. heavy cream
4 tblsp. sifted confectioners sugar

Beat egg whites in large bowl at high speed until frothy. Add salt and cream of tartar; beat until stiff peaks form. Gradually add sugar, beating well until soft glossy peaks form. Blend in vanilla.

Sift cake flour over egg white mixture in 4 equal parts; fold in carefully.

Beat egg yolks in bowl until thick and lemon-colored (about 5 minutes). Fold egg yolks into egg white mixture. Pour batter into ungreased 10-inch tube pan. Pull metal spatula through batter once to break large air bubbles.

Bake in 325° oven 1 hour 15 minutes or until cake tests done. Invert tube pan on funnel or bottle to cool. When completely cooled, remove from pan.

Cut cake into 5 layers. Prepare Chocolate Spice Filling and Lemon Fruit Filling. Fill layers alternately with fillings.

Whip cream in bowl until it starts to thicken. Gradually add confectioners sugar, beating until soft peaks form. Frost tops and sides of cake. Chill several hours. Makes 12 servings.

Chocolate Spice Filling: Prepare 1 (3¾ oz.) pkg. chocolate pudding and pie filling according to package directions, using 1½ c. milk and adding ½ tsp. ground cinnamon. Cover and cool to room temperature. Whip ½ c. heavy cream; fold into pudding. Add 2 tblsp. slivered toasted almonds. Chill 15 minutes.

Lemon Fruit Filling: Prepare 1 (3¼ oz.) pkg. vanilla pudding and pie filling according to package directions, using 1½ c. milk. Cover and cool to room temperature. Add 2 tsp. lemon juice and 1 tblsp. grated lemon rind. Whip ½ c. heavy cream until stiff; fold into pudding. Add ⅓ c. drained pineapple tidbits and ¼ c. drained, quartered red maraschino cherries. Chill 15 minutes.

CHOCOLATE ICE CREAM ROLL

½ c. sugar
¼ c. sifted flour
¼ c. baking cocoa
¼ tsp. salt
5 egg whites
½ tsp. cream of tartar
½ c. sugar
5 egg yolks
1 tsp. vanilla
1 qt. vanilla ice cream, softened

Sift together ½ c. sugar, flour, cocoa and salt twice.

Beat egg whites and cream of tartar in bowl until foamy. Gradually beat in ½ c. sugar.

Beat egg yolks and vanilla in another bowl until thick and lemon-colored. Fold sifted dry ingredients into yolk mixture. Then carefully fold yolk mixture into beaten whites. Pour into greased and waxed paper-lined 15½x10½x1-inch jelly roll pan.

Bake in 325° oven about 25 minutes. Immediately turn out onto towel sprinkled with confectioners sugar. Roll cake as for jelly roll, from narrow side. Cool thoroughly.

Unroll cake, quickly spread with softened ice cream. Roll up again. Wrap in aluminum foil or clear plastic. Freeze. Cut in slices to serve. Makes about 8 servings.

MOCHA-NUT TORTE

2½ c. sifted flour
2 tsp. baking powder
1 tsp. baking soda
½ tsp. salt
1 tblsp. instant coffee powder
1 c. butter
2 c. sugar
4 egg yolks, well beaten
1 c. warm mashed potatoes
2 (1 oz.) squares unsweetened chocolate, melted and cooled slightly
1 tsp. vanilla
1 c. buttermilk
1 c. finely chopped walnuts
4 egg whites, stiffly beaten
6 tblsp. butter
3 (1 oz.) squares unsweetened chocolate
2 c. sifted confectioners sugar
1 tsp. instant coffee powder
¼ c. milk
2 eggs
1 tsp. vanilla

Sift together flour, baking powder, baking soda, salt, and 1 tblsp. coffee powder.

Cream together 1 c. butter and sugar in large bowl until light and fluffy. Beat in egg yolks, potatoes and 2 squares chocolate. Add 1 tsp. vanilla to buttermilk. Add dry ingredients alternately with buttermilk to egg yolk mixture. Stir in walnuts. Gently fold in egg whites. Pour into 9-inch well-greased spring form or 10-inch tube pan with removable bottom.

Bake in 350° oven about 1 hour. Cool thoroughly; remove from pan. Frost immediately or freeze for later use and frost at time of serving.

Melt together 6 tblsp. butter and 3 squares chocolate in saucepan; cool. Combine confectioners sugar, 1 tsp. coffee powder, milk, 2 eggs and 1 tsp. vanilla in well-chilled bowl. Add chocolate mixture; beat on high speed of electric mixer until frosting is fluffy and of good spreading consistency. Spread on torte. Refrigerate. Makes 20 to 24 servings.

PINEAPPLE CHEESECAKE

1¼ c. crushed zwieback crumbs
2 tblsp. sugar
2 tblsp. melted butter
4 egg yolks, well beaten
2 (8 oz.) pkgs. cream cheese, softened
1 tsp. vanilla
½ c. sugar
2 tblsp. flour
¼ tsp. salt
1 c. light cream
4 egg whites
¼ tsp. salt
½ c. well-drained crushed pineapple

Blend zwieback crumbs with 2 tblsp. sugar and melted butter in bowl. Reserve ¼ c. mixture for topping. Press remaining crumb mixture on bottom and about 1 inch up sides of 9-inch spring form pan.

Beat together egg yolks, cream cheese and vanilla in large bowl until mixture is smooth and fluffy. Combine ½ c. sugar, flour and ¼ tsp. salt; slowly add to cream cheese mixture, beating constantly. Stir in light cream, a little at a time, beating well.

Combine egg whites and ¼ tsp. salt in bowl. Beat until stiff but not dry. Fold beaten egg whites, with drained pineapple, gently but thoroughly into cheese mixture. Turn into crumb-lined pan and top with reserved crumbs.

Bake in 325° oven 1½ hours or until filling is set. Remove from oven; cool 30 minutes. Loosen cheesecake from sides of pan and cool 30 minutes more. Release spring form, remove rim and chill cheesecake on pan bottom at least 5 to 6 hours. Makes 12 to 16 servings.

CHAPTER IX

Hints and Helps

Planning Oven Meals

● Apply basic menu planning rules:

Consider flavor. Include some foods which complement and others that contrast with the main dish. Gentle oven heat preserves and enhances food flavors, gives them a chance to blend during baking. Toasting or browning gives special taste appeal.

Vary texture and temperature. A meal is more interesting if you plan some soft foods, some crisp and chewy or crunchy textures. And, for a variety, serve a chilled appetizer or salad, or end a hot-from-the-oven meal with a refreshing frosty dessert.

Be color conscious. Coordinate colors in menus. Bright red tomatoes or apples, red cranberries or beets, rosy pink ham, green and yellow vegetables, can liven a meal.

Vary food shapes. Different shapes add to the appearance of a meal. Include, for example, sliced roast beef, browned whole potatoes, diced carrots, asparagus spears as a salad, a scoop of ice cream or a wedge of pie for dessert. Avoid too many mixtures in the same meal.

● Consider the oven for:

Some of your slow cooking top-of-range favorites like pot roast, Swiss steak or braised beef shanks. Make them the basis of an oven meal, and let the oven eliminate the pot watching for you.

Heating frozen foods like stew, soup or chili. No minding or stirring on your part. Put other foods in the oven to bake alongside, either to serve with them or later.

Meats and poultry you've usually fried. Besides reducing calories, you'll save precious time.

French toast. You'll like its light texture and the delicate flavor. And you'll cut a few calories, too.

Preparation Tricks

• If you already have the oven on, use it for melting the butter, margarine, shortening or chocolate called for in a recipe instead of turning on a surface unit. Use a long-handled measuring cup in place of a custard cup or other smooth-surfaced dish to hold the butter or other ingredient. It's much easier to grasp when hot and you'll be less likely to spill the contents.

• Spread slivered or chopped almonds or other nuts on a cookie sheet and toast in your oven when it's already in use for something else. If the oven is set between 300° and 375° F., the nuts will take about 15 to 20 minutes. Stir occasionally to toast evenly.

Or, after you've turned off a hot oven (400° F. or more), slip the pan of nuts in and let them toast slowly in stored heat.

• Toast coconut the same way. Toasting time will vary with the moisture of the coconut, so watch carefully.

• After removing food, take advantage of a still-hot oven by drying bread for crumbs or celery leaves for seasoning, or by crisping frozen cookies for dessert.

• Heat dinner plates, soup mugs or bowls in a still toasty-warm oven before serving food.

Meat Cookery Tips

• Bake thick beef patties to a beautiful deep brown outside and pink and juicy inside. Place them in an oiled shallow pan and bake in a 400°F. oven. Patties of 1-inch thickness will take about 20 minutes.

• Bake bacon, instead of pan-frying, for convenience and for good eating. Lay strips, fat edge of one strip slightly overlapping lean of next one, on a rack in a shallow pan. Bake on top rack of 400° F. oven for 12 to 15 minutes, until it's the crispness you like. No watching, no turning or draining!

• Oven-sear chops, pot roasts and Swiss steak in oven at 425° F. instead of browning on top of range. Then add seasoning and a small amount of liquid, cover and finish baking at 325° F.

• To protect neck cavity and drumsticks of poultry from overbrowning during roasting, cover loosely with pieces of aluminum foil.

• If you want to bake poultry the old-fashioned "covered roaster" style, use heavy-duty foil over the entire bird, crimping the foil tightly to the edges of the pan.

• Depend on a meat thermometer—or the automatic thermometer on your range—to tell you the exact degree of doneness of a roast.

• To thaw solidly frozen ground beef for use in combination dishes, place in shallow pan in a 425° F. oven. As the outer surface thaws, break the meat off with a fork and push to bottom of the pan. Continue until entire chunk is thawed, stirring meat to brown lightly and evenly. Combine with other ingredients promptly, or refrigerate and use later that day.

Tips on Bakeware

• Bright shiny aluminum pans are usually best for even browning of breads, cakes and cookies. If the pans have darkened, they are likely to cause overbrowning.

• Anodized aluminum pans have an oxide, with or without color, deposited on the surface. It absorbs heat

147

quickly, gives a very brown bottom crust to such products as breads and pies.

• Glass or glass-ceramic bakeware (Pyroceram) absorbs and holds heat very well, allowing you to reduce the oven temperature by 25 degrees from the normal baking temperature.

• Pyroceram tolerates extremes of temperature, can go non-stop from freezer to oven. It's great for freezing casserole mixtures and then baking right in the same pan.

• The size and shape of cake pans affects the volume and texture of baked cake. In too small a pan, the batter runs over; in too large a pan, it's shallow in the pan and overbakes. If a pan is warped or badly dented, the cake will rise and brown unevenly.

• Give cookie and other baking sheets enough "elbow room" on oven racks—2 inches on all sides for good heat circulation and even browning.

• Although Teflon has been improved to be harder and more resistant to scratching than when originally introduced, avoid sharp metal utensils when using any Teflon-lined bakeware. Protect it against scratches from other untensils when stacking it in the sink before dishwashing and when you store it.

Oven Know-How

• Check your oven periodically with a reliable oven thermometer to see that the thermostat is accurate. If it's off, have it regulated by a service man.

• Arrange racks before turning on the oven. If using only one, divide the oven in half; if using two, divide the oven in thirds.

• Stagger pans or baking dishes on racks, so that no pan or dish is directly over another.

• Use two baking sheets in a 30-inch oven, if you like,

and switch them from one rack to the other halfway through the baking period.

● For even browning, be sure pans don't touch—each other, the oven walls or the door.

● Set your minute timer 4 or 5 minutes before the scheduled end of baking time, so you can check the product and guard against over baking.

● Whether it's a self-cleaning or a regular standard oven, make the job easier by cleaning before it becomes excessively dirty.

Freezing Baked Foods

● Keep in mind that a freezer can only preserve food quality—and for a limited time. It cannot improve it.

● Insure best possible keeping quality by using packaging materials which will protect the food from moisture loss and, in the case of baked goods, protect them against crushing and breakage.

● If you're storing food for less than 2 months, the freezer wrap which is waxed on only one side is adequate (but not waxed paper).

● Best protection for longer storage is offered by materials which are air-moisture-vapor proof. These include heavy-duty aluminum foil, foil laminated to a paper base, plastic wrap, and some of the polyester and combination films. They're available in sheet form and/or as bags and sometimes cartons.

● Seal packages firmly with freezer tape, and use a good marking pencil to properly identify the contents. Include the weight or number of servings and the date.

● Work out an inventory system, so you'll know what's on hand and can use foods when they're at their peak quality.

Do's and Don'ts

- DO utilize every bit of rack space when you're using the oven. Fill empty spots with a dish of dried fruit, to steam for breakfast or to use in a dessert compote; a pan of baking apples or pears; a few potatoes or a winter squash; some bread to dry for crumbs. Choose your "rack filler" according to the temperature you're using.
- DO use the size casserole or baking dish called for in your recipe. Otherwise, baking time is likely to be different from that given in the recipe.
- DO, if you have a conventional oven, wipe out the oven with warm sudsy water after each use, and especially after broiling or roasting meat or poultry, then rinse well and dry. Saves a big oven-cleaning job later.
- DON'T cover floor or the racks of the oven with aluminum foil unless the "use and care " booklet for your particular range suggests it. Doing so can interfere with heat circulation and browning.

To catch potential bubble-overs from a casserole, a pie or pudding, place a piece of foil, just slightly larger than the baking dish and with edges turned up all around, on the rack below it.

- DON'T open and close the oven door too frequently during the baking period. You lose oven heat and, with some foods, may interfere with their proper baking.
- DON'T forget the tried-and-true ammonia method for cleaning a conventional oven. Pour ½ c. household ammonia, plain or lemon scented, into a dish and let it stand in the cold oven overnight, with the doors closed. In the morning, the soil will have softened and will be easy to remove with warm sudsy water. Then rinse and dry. (You may have to remove stubborn burned-on spots with a soap-filled pad.)
- DON'T ever use oven cleaners, harsh abrasives or soap-filled pads on self-cleaning ovens.

Index

151

153